PRAISE FOR *THE HACKER MINDSET*

"You don't have to have a degree in computer science or be a Unix command line wizard for this book to change your life. Garrett brilliantly distills the skills and frameworks hackers have mastered with computers and teaches you how to leverage them to build a rich life, a gratifying and lucrative career, dynamic relationships, and much more. Highly recommended!"

—Andrew Youderian, Founder, eCommerceFuel

"Garrett will teach you the tools and techniques to reverse-engineer your life so that you can achieve more than you could've ever imagined. Armed with his firsthand knowledge, you can craft the life you want using *The Hacker Mindset* approach to life."

—Jim Wang, WalletHacks.com

"Garrett's *The Hacker Mindset* is a compelling read for anyone who wants to apply the hacker's agile and innovative approach to life, work, and everything in between."

—Peter Kim, Author, The Hacker Playbook series

"A book that hits differently. *The Hacker Mindset* has re-imagined the building blocks of productivity. As a fellow author, 1 admire how Garrett has woven intricate hacker strategies into the fabric of everyday effectiveness."

—Peter Hollins, Internationally Bestselling Author

"With *The Hacker Mindset*, Garrett has crafted an essential guide for anyone eager to disrupt their own status quo and hack their way to success."

—Ian Schoen, Cofounder, Dynamite Circle

"Garrett Gee's *The Hacker Mindset* is a must-read for business leaders seeking a fresh perspective on problem-solving and creative thinking in the corporate world."

—Andrew Hutton, Founder and Venture Builder

THE HACKER
M!NDSET

THE HACKER
MINDSET

A 5-Step Methodology
for Cracking the System and
Achieving Your Dreams

GARRETT GEE

Matt Holt Books
An Imprint of BenBella Books, Inc.
Dallas, TX

Matt Holt is an imprint of BenBella Books, Inc.
10440 N. Central Expressway
Suite 800
Dallas, TX 75231
benbellabooks.com
Send feedback to feedback@benbellabooks.com

BenBella and *Matt Holt* are federally registered trademarks.

Printed in the United States of America
10 9 8 7 6 5 4 3 2 1

Library of Congress Control Number: 2023048511
ISBN 9781637744864 (hardcover)
ISBN 9781637744871 (electronic)

Editing by Katie Dickman
Copyediting by Michael Fedison
Proofreading by Doug Johnson and Becky Maines
Text design and composition by Aaron Edmiston
Cover design by Brigid Pearson
Printed by Lake Book Manufacturing

Special discounts for bulk sales are available.
Please contact bulkorders@benbellabooks.com.

To the future hackers of the world

and

To Melanie, Ryan, Stephanie, Samantha, Ashley, Zoe, and Owen

CONTENTS

PART III—THE HACKER MINDSET APPLIED

FOREWORD

Hi friends,

I'm thrilled to introduce you to *The Hacker Mindset*, a book that resonates deeply with my passion for productivity and personal development. This isn't your typical tech-centric read; it's a universal guide, perfect for students, professionals, entrepreneurs, and anyone aiming to master their life.

Garrett's concept of applying a hacker's perspective to everyday challenges is both refreshing and thought provoking. *The Hacker Mindset* isn't about hacking computers; it's about hacking life. It teaches you to see the world like a hacker sees a system—full of opportunities to understand, navigate, and, ultimately, reshape to your advantage. This perspective can dramatically boost your efficiency and success in various aspects of life.

The Hacker Mindset covers a wide range of hacking topics, creating a cohesive toolbox that enables anyone to adopt the hacker's philosophy. From reverse engineering and resourcefulness to risk-taking and social engineering, Garrett provides strategies and insights that will change how you approach life's challenges and opportunities. It matches well with my mantra of working smarter, not just harder.

In essence, *The Hacker Mindset* is a guide to breaking the mold. It pushes you to think differently, challenges the status quo, equips you with unconventional strategies, and inspires you to achieve more than just "good enough." I highly recommend it to anyone eager to step up their game and embark on a journey toward remarkable achievement.

So, if you're up for a challenge and ready to look at life through a new, exciting lens, embrace the hacker mindset and watch as the possibilities unfold before you.

Wishing you all the best on your hacking journey,

Ali Abdaal
YouTuber and author of *Feel-Good Productivity*

INTRODUCTION

Steve Jobs stood at ease onstage, his hands held loosely at his side, the Apple logo silhouetted on a huge screen behind him. He spoke slowly and confidently, allowing his words to settle upon the audience. He was building up to something big—I could see it in his eyes.

It was January 2007 and I was at Macworld, sitting in the front row for Steve Jobs's keynote speech. I fiddled idly with the VIP badge that hung from a lanyard around my neck as I watched him draw out his words.

"This is a day," he said, "I've been looking forward to for two and a half years."

Cheers erupted around me and I joined the applause. Jobs continued to recount Apple's history of developing revolutionary products and was greeted with even greater cheers. The enthusiasm was infectious and I found myself yelling along with the rest of them as he listed each product. He talked about the Macintosh and the iPod, but then silence descended upon the auditorium as we all speculated on what new innovation was about to be revealed. Steve Jobs, smiling knowingly, allowed the silence to stretch out.

"An iPod," he said, "a phone, and an internet communicator."

He repeated the words again and again, the cheers growing louder and louder as the penny dropped that he wasn't talking about three different products, but one. Finally, raising his voice to be heard over the shouts and ongoing applause, he said the words that would dispel all doubt.

"This is one device, and we are calling it iPhone."

The auditorium shook with roars of unfettered joy and the stage was illuminated by the flash of countless cameras as the press rushed to capture this iconic moment. I took that moment to look about. All around me sat Apple executives and high-level industry participants. Crammed together, lining the sides of the room, were journalists and photographers from all the major media outlets. Far away at the back of the room, Apple fans stood shoulder to shoulder, straining their eyes to follow Steve Jobs's form on the stage.

And then there was me. I wasn't an Apple executive or a leader in the tech world. I wasn't a member of the press or even much of an Apple fan. I hadn't written out a huge check to get into the expo as some of the people sitting beside me had; in fact, I hadn't paid a single penny. Nevertheless, there I was, sitting in the front row of what may have been the biggest tech reveal of my lifetime, the badge around my neck assuring everyone that I was a VIP.

How did I get there? It was so simple. A couple of months earlier I, along with a research partner of mine, had discovered a vulnerability in the Macworld website. Having hacked the system, it was easy to attain top-tier passes to the event for free. We chuckled as we granted ourselves those front-row tickets—attending the event was going to be fun.

And so there I was, having a blast hanging around with top-level Apple executives, knowing I could hack my way into just about any-thing I wanted. Watching Steve Jobs walk back and forth onstage in his trademark turtleneck, I felt like the king of the world. I should have known that feeling wouldn't last. Even as I made my way home from the event, back to my day job, I began to wonder whether I was really the one who had come out on top. Sure, I'd hacked my way into Macworld to sit alongside the bigwigs of the tech industry, but I wasn't sitting on a million-dollar salary like they were.

For the following few weeks these thoughts ran round and round my mind, and my mood came crashing down. At the time I had a pretty good job, but I would have been lying to myself if I'd said I was happy with where I was. I was smart, I was talented, I was just about as good a hacker as you could find, but receiving my next paycheck hammered home just how underappreciated my abilities were. What was wrong with me? How could it be that I was able to hack the Macworld system and get myself into the iPhone-reveal expo, yet remain so mediocre in my professional life? How had I become so stuck?

It would take me a couple of years to answer these questions.

IN THE BELLY OF THE MACHINE

Most people live their lives trapped in systems so intricate they can't see them for what they are. Companies, societies, and even governments resemble huge machines, with individual people forming their components. And, just like in a machine, each component works hard in performing a role, but the ultimate result of all that work is determined by the machine itself and not by its constituent parts.

The systems of our world are so complex that they even give the people inside them the illusion of choice. Different paths open up before them—a potential promotion or a new job offer, for example. It's almost like being in a maze, but the irony is that in this maze there is no way out. The machine needs all its components working toward its goal. No matter which path an individual takes, as long as they are trapped in the belly of the machine, they'll be no closer to achieving their own goals.

That's exactly how it was for me. At the age of fifteen, after being put forward by two of my teachers, I was offered a job at a Sandia

National Laboratories (a federally funded research lab), and for me it was a no-brainer to accept. Nearly all my family had worked in public services; it was seen to be a secure and reliable career; and it helped that the lab itself was only a thirty-minute drive from where I lived. So, there I was, in an office full of PhD graduates and computer geniuses tasked with building up the cybersecurity industry from scratch. Exciting, right? When other fifteen-year-olds were busy playing Pogs and video games, I was becoming a tech pioneer. I was a literal boy genius. In 2000, the crew of *60 Minutes* flew to California to interview me and I ended up on national television as a hacking expert. Fame and fortune seemed to be at my doorstep.

That's how it should have been. But as the years went on and I progressed in my career, I began to feel more and more trapped. By this time I'd moved from the national lab to work for the Federal Reserve Bank, but deep inside I could sense that something was wrong. The work I was doing was interesting—groundbreaking, even—but it was becoming clear to me that I was just another employee, receiving one paycheck after the other.

There wasn't much upward growth where I worked. Promotions were available and I achieved a few, but none of these would really alter the state of my life in any drastic way. I became more senior, got slightly better pay, but in reality I was still just laboring away at the same old grindstone. As far as my career went, I was reaching a point of diminishing returns—no matter how much effort I put into excelling at my job, I wasn't receiving much more in terms of salary for myself. It was the Federal Reserve that was reaping the true rewards of my work, not me.

I was really a model employee. I worked hard, went above and beyond, earned my pay, and saved a little money from my paycheck each month. I was the paragon of the American work ethic, the exemplar of the "sensible" worker. But when looking at my life more broadly, I couldn't help but wonder, *What am I doing?* Working, earning, saving, working, earning, saving, on and on as I propelled myself toward a comfortable and unremarkable retirement. It almost made me sick to think about it. There I was, brain bursting with talent, having achieved so much, having been one of the small group of people who built the cybersecurity industry *from scratch*, and all I really amounted to was another cog in the machine.

This was all running through the back of my mind one morning as I led a meeting of my team, allowing my cup of coffee to grow cold while I answered various questions. I was almost operating on autopilot. Eventually I dismissed my team and took a sip of my cold coffee as I watched them file out of the room.

Is this really it?

The thought forced its way to the surface of my mind. I couldn't ignore it. Despite my hacking prowess, I was unsatisfied with the state of my life. Years after hacking my way into the big iPhone reveal, I was just as stuck as ever.

Was the life I was living really the life of a hacker? As I was about to discover, the answer was a resounding *no*. But then what did it mean to be a hacker? That's what we're going to find out over the course of this book.

ESCAPING THE MACHINE

Hacking is generally thought of as a dark and seditious business. When most people think of a hacker they imagine a shady character, hidden away in a basement, face bathed in the green light of computer screens. We imagine Neo and Trinity from *The Matrix*, or the unnumbered members of Anonymous, their identities concealed behind Guy Fawkes masks. Though these images of hackers are pretty specific and certainly exaggerated, they do contain a core truth that also lies at the heart of this book:

Hacking is about manipulating systems to get what you want, as quickly and efficiently as possible.

It's about identifying the barriers between yourself and your goals and determining the fastest way to overcome them. While in the context of cybersecurity the systems you manipulate are computer programs, the approach can be applied more broadly.

Back in my office at the Federal Reserve I mused upon this as I poured out my cold coffee and made a fresh cup. All those skills and that knowledge I'd used throughout my career, manipulating systems like I did with Macworld: Could I take those principles and apply them to my own life?

I could feel the excitement bubble up in my body as I worked it out in my head. I could hack computers by understanding their underlying systems. Life was also full of systems. All I had to do was understand the underlying systems in my own life, work out their variables and parameters, and bingo—I'd be on an express train to success. It then became clear how I could escape from the belly of the machine. Rather than continue to walk along the myriad paths presented to me by the maze, I could break through the walls, climb over them, and escape the maze entirely to forge my own path.

In the following months I crystallized these ideas and used them as the basis to create an ecommerce business within my existing industry I called Hacker Warehouse. I tested the model via a pop-up store during a three-day industry event, and within the first two hours I'd sold out my entire inventory. Clearly, I was on to something special. This was the moment when it all started to happen for me. I spent more and more time building up my business, eventually quitting my day job to dedicate myself to it full time, ready at last to work toward my own goals rather than those the machine put before me.

Five years later, business was booming and I was doing $1 million in revenue. I'd moved to classy new offices in Southern California and my prominence in the industry was so high that I was being asked to participate in shows such as *Mr. Robot* and *Sense8*. Just a few years earlier I had been an employee, had a team of twelve working for me, and was working hard for a fairly modest paycheck. Now I was a successful business owner, taking in seven figures, and working only seven hours a week.

What astounded me most wasn't what I was doing; it was that I hadn't done it sooner!

In retrospect everything seems obvious, but for years I had been laboring away with all the skills I needed to become successful in my own right, but never applying them in the correct way. I had been so trapped in the machine of life that I couldn't see the systems around me. Now my eyes are open and the path to success is clear. Now that I've applied the hacker mindset to my own life, I want to help others do the same. I want to teach you the hacker principles and show you how to use them to fast-track your life to success.

With the hacker mindset in place, you will see the possibilities unfold before you. What is the hacker mindset? Well, read on to find out!

THE GOALS OF THIS BOOK

For so many people, life is "good enough." They make a decent living and live comfortable lives—what more could they ask for? For others, however, "good enough" simply isn't good enough. If you recognize yourself in that description, then this book is for you. If you consider yourself smart and want to learn how to overcome the systems around you to achieve true success, then this book is for you.

Going through this book, you will learn how to pursue your goals in three stages:

1. You will learn how hackers see the world in terms of systems to be overcome, and about some of the key characteristics hackers exhibit in doing so. These perspectives and characteristics make up the hacker mindset, which you, too, can adopt.

2. You will learn all about the six hacker principles and how they can be put into practice using the hacker methodology.
3. You will learn how you can apply the hacker mindset in a variety of real-life contexts, including in your career, business, and personal finance.

If you feel that you're stuck in life, this book will show you how to become unstuck. If you've become trapped in a job that doesn't excite you, this book will show you how to escape. If you've become frustrated with the lack of progress in your life, this book will show you how to ascend into the stratosphere.

The machine of life is designed to make people feel that things are "acceptable." The hacker mindset will show you that you need not settle for "acceptable," and show you just how far beyond that you can go.

Finally, and before we begin, I just want to make one thing clear: this is an amoral book. The principles of hacking are powerful and I'm not here to tell you how to make use of them.

In the world of cybersecurity, you can find all types of hackers. You find the "black-hat hackers" who cross the moral line and use their hacking abilities to steal valuable information or to hold companies ransom. On the other side there are the "ethical hackers" who use their talents to help companies protect themselves from virtual attacks. Then there are the "console cowboys" who break their way into systems simply to cause chaos and make life difficult for everyone.

They're all hackers, they all have the same skill sets, but they choose to use them in very different ways.

The purpose of *The Hacker Mindset* is to give you the tools you need to expertly maneuver the systems around you and determine the best decisions you can make toward your goals. Being the ethical person you are, you probably won't use these skills to lie, cheat, and steal your way to success, but ultimately that choice lies with you and I will not be holding anything back. At the end of the day, it comes down to this quote from Nir Eyal that I'm quite fond of: "If you couldn't use it for evil, it wouldn't be a superpower."

Now let's get hacking.

Part I

THE HACKER
MINDSET

Chapter 1

THE WORLD IS MADE OF SYSTEMS

It was a sunny spring morning in 1991 when I, along with around three hundred of my fellow elementary school classmates, sat on the grass in the playground. An excited hubbub arose from the crowd, slowly growing in intensity. This was a moment we'd been anticipating all week, and eager chatter flowed freely. For my part I remained silent—I didn't want to give anything away.

Two of my teachers and the principal of the school emerged onto the podium that had been erected before us. They were carrying a big red box that was filled to the brim with little yellow slips of paper, and they ceremoniously placed the box down. The idea was quite simple. Each slip of paper bore the name of a student. Every time a student exhibited good behavior, a teacher would award them a slip of paper with their name on it, which they'd then place in the box. Then, at the end of each week, a name would be drawn from the box and that person would win that week's prize.

It was a pretty elegant system. The better behaved a student had been, the more slips with their name would be in the box and so the better their chance of winning would be, but at the same time anyone who had been good at all had a chance of winning. This reward system was meant to reflect the real world, where hard work would always pay off, but was also always augmented with a little luck. As it turned out, it was a much better reflection of the real world than the teachers had anticipated.

A silence descended on us as the principal raised her hands. She spoke briefly, emphasizing the importance of us being there and reminding us that good behavior would give us the best chance of winning the prize. I couldn't help the grin that spread across my face upon hearing her words. She turned to the teacher at her side and beckoned her to the box.

"Would you please do the honors and draw the winner?" she asked.

A roar of excitement burst up from the crowd as the teacher took up the box and held it up for us to see. I think at that moment each one of my classmates was imagining themself climbing up onto the podium to accept the prize. I knew that for me there would no need to only imagine. As the teacher reached into the box, we all fell quiet. She pulled out a slip of paper.

Shock washed over her face. She stood there motionless for a few moments and I could almost see the gears whirring in her head as she tried to puzzle it out. She fell back to the others on the podium and showed them the slip. The other teacher mouthed a single word: *Again?* The principal looked at both of them and after a couple of seconds shrugged her shoulders. The rules were the rules and a name had been pulled out of the box.

My teacher stepped back up to the microphone, cleared her throat, and, with a notable lack of enthusiasm, began to speak.

"This week's winner," she said, "is Garrett Gee."

Whispered consternation spread through the students. *Did she say Garrett? No, it can't have been! Really, Garrett!?* A couple of my more easygoing classmates began to clap, but the applause didn't catch on. The teachers had stopped smiling and were looking at me with suspicious frowns as they quickly clambered up to the podium. They thrust the prize into my hands and hurriedly sent us back to class.

I couldn't really blame everyone for their less-than-enthusiastic reaction to my win. I'd won the prize the previous week as well. And the week before that. In fact, this was the sixth week in a row that I'd won the prize for good behavior. And I knew that I was going to keep on winning it for weeks to come.

How could I be so sure that I'd win? Well, if you bear with me for a few more pages, I'll tell you.

RECOGNIZING THE SYSTEMS

Key to my success at the good behavior prize draw at school was the recognition that the world is full of systems. Things rarely happen completely randomly and are instead usually based on predictable systems. In fact, perceived randomness is more often than not merely a consequence of a lack of knowledge about the underlying systems, and understanding those systems is the key to making them work in your favor. Take for example a simple die. When you roll the die, you have no idea what number is going to show up. But if you had all the information about how the die was rolled, such as the force and direction with which it was thrown and the angle at which it hit the surface, you could predict the number that would come up every time.

Of course, it's not reasonably possible to know precisely how a die is thrown, so that event remains for all intents and purposes random, but this is not the case for so many of the other and more important "random" events in our lives. Recognizing this has led to one of the most important maxims of my life: look for the hidden systems.

To exemplify this, let's consider a scenario. Let's say that you're someone who's just starting out in a career in the tech industry and are looking to build up your network and connect with prominent figures in the industry. You're looking for people who are widely lauded for their intelligence, insight, and experience. Someone you can connect with on a personal level. Someone who won't just see you as another fan, but as an individual who could become just as prominent in the industry as they are.

Searching on Google, you find that Mark Cuban is giving the keynote speech at a conference in three weeks' time. He's a perfect connection—a superstar in the tech industry. You set your sights on networking with Mark Cuban. But how exactly would you go about it?

In the world of hacking this is called "gaining access." How would you gain access to Mark Cuban?

The conference is not very far from where you live. After his speech he'll be giving a Q&A session where he fields questions from anyone in the audience. You could get into the conference and come up with a question so intelligent and insightful that he'll have to take notice of you. However, the cost of attending the conference is $2,000 and even if you get in there's no guarantee that you'll get to ask your question. There'll be hundreds of other keen industry participants in the room during the Q&A, each one of them eager to put their questions to Mark Cuban. But as things stand, attending the Q&A seems like your best bet.

This is what is known as "expected behavior." Most people will take this approach, shelling out the $2,000 and hoping that they stand out from the crowd. And the more people that go down this route, the less likely it becomes for any one individual to succeed. The more you consider it, the less promising the situation looks, but these are the parameters that are presented to you.

The majority of people will determine that they'll have to work really hard within these parameters to increase their chances of success. Maybe they'll get to the conference early and make sure they're at the front of the queue for the microphone when the Q&A starts. The fact is, however, that most if not all of these people will end up making a very limited impact on Mark Cuban.

If you're a hacker you'll approach the scenario differently, recognizing first and foremost that there is a system underlying the conference, with multiple other systems running in tandem. By identifying these systems and understanding their rules and processes, you can learn how to take advantage of them and maximize your chances of connecting with Mark Cuban.

You'll approach the situation applying the six principles of the hacker mindset. First off, you'll **be on offense** (Hacker Principle 1), being proactive and ensuring that you are the one making the decisions. You'll undertake **reverse engineering** (Hacker Principle 2), looking at the situation from all the different angles to determine the various options available to you beyond the most obvious ones. You'll **live off the land** (Hacker Principle 3), taking advantage of freely available resources to maximize your chances of success. You will calculate **risk** (Hacker Principle 4), reviewing all the options and factors and determining what will be most likely to get you what you want with as little cost and effort as possible, and engage in **social engineering** (Hacker Principle 5), making use of people to achieve your goal. Finally, you will **pivot** (Hacker Principle 6), approaching the problem from different angles and reacting to the changing factors in the scenario.

Over the course of this book I'll expound upon each of these principles, but for now let's see how things might turn out if you apply Hacker Principle 2: Reverse Engineering. You take a deep look into the conference's website, phone a few friends who might have some more information about it, and call up the organizer of the conference and ask a few questions. You compile all this information and then all of a sudden you find you have plenty of choices before you.

While you were operating within the parameters of expected behavior, you really only had one option:

> Spend $2,000 on a ticket and hope that Mark Cuban notices you in the Q&A.

After applying Hacker Principle 2, you find that you can:

- Find a promo code and buy the ticket at a discounted price (limited access, cheaper entry price).
- Volunteer to help out facilitating the event (different access, cheaper entry price, less time available for the event itself).
- Help out the catering company in order to get access to Mark Cuban during meals (different access, cheaper entry price).
- Pay for a VIP ticket for front-row seating and guaranteed face time (different access, higher entry price).
- Become a speaker at the event and meet Mark Cuban backstage (better access, different entry price).
- Collect press credentials and get a media kit to prepare for the event, a press-related Q&A, and dedicated one-on-one time with Mark Cuban (better access, cheaper entry price).
- Arrange a "random" run-in at Mark Cuban's airport, hotel, or favorite coffee shop while he's in town (potential better access, cheaper entry price).

Clearly I'm making some assumptions with this list of options, but in all likelihood you would end up with a similar list of options after doing your own reverse engineering. Of course, some options are better than others, some are more likely to get you what you want than others, and some come with bigger costs or risks. Now you have multiple avenues to go down, and whereas previously you were stuck with a game of chance, you can now exert more control over the results you attain based on the options you choose. In short, by recognizing the underlying systems, you've given yourself more power to determine your own destiny.

And the fact is that nearly everything is structured as a system. Buying a Tesla is a system. Here the expected behavior is to check the website haphazardly, hoping there will be some availability near where you live. But with the hacker mindset you could have a simple tool developed that would scan availability of Teslas in various areas every couple of minutes, and have an SMS sent to your phone as soon as one becomes available. Instead of waiting months for a Tesla, you can get one in a couple of days.

You could also hack the system that underlies getting hired. Follow the expected behavior here and you'll wear yourself out sending countless resumés to innumerable companies, hoping that you'll hear back from one or two and perhaps get an interview. Hack the system and you'll recognize that hundreds of applications are dismissed at the first stage by an algorithm, prompting you to use the correct key words in the correct order to get past that first hurdle. Or you could hack the system in another way by building the right relations with the right hiring managers and dispensing with sending in resumés altogether.

Even retirement is a system that can be hacked. The onslaught of information about index funds, ETFs, 401(k)s, and the like can be overwhelming and super confusing. But when it comes down to it, it's all just a matter of math, which is completely systematic. Do the math right and you could find yourself retiring as early as fifty, forty, or even thirty.

The moment you decide to abandon expected behavior and to manipulate the systems rather than working within their parameters, you'll find that your options become almost limitless. It's just a matter of breaking down the systems in question and making them work to your advantage.

SYSTEMS, SYSTEMS EVERYWHERE

The whole world is made of systems. Everywhere humans go, they create rules and mechanisms in an attempt to make life a little easier—in short, they create civilization. All societies are made up of a collection of laws, conventions, and habits. When you work within these, you're just like everyone else. But if you learn to transcend these systems, you'll be able to distinguish yourself as a cut above the rest.

Of course, some systems have higher stakes than others. If you fail to pay your income tax, for example, you're almost certainly going to get into a lot of trouble with the IRS. Other systems can be escaped but are so huge and complicated it can be difficult to see how. In chapter eleven, we'll look at one such system, the system of a corporation, and learn exactly how it can be broken down and taken advantage of.

Other systems are smaller and simpler. Some might even be thought of as banal, such as the system underlying the weekly good-behavior prize at my elementary school. Most people would probably think it a system undeserving of a second thought, but as a ten-year-old I wanted those prizes and so I was determined to beat the system.

The teachers had designed it so that every student would have a fair chance of winning the prize, so long as they behaved well. Good behavior came naturally to me and I did get many tickets with my name on them to place in the box for the drawing. But then I wasn't the only well-behaved student in the school, and operating within the system I would only be as likely to win the prize as some of those other students. So what could I do to better ensure I would win the reward?

I realized one day that my teachers never shuffled the tickets when they drew a name for the prize. They would just stick an arm into the box and pull out the first name that came to hand. All I had to do was wait until the last minute before putting my tickets in the box and I would ensure that my name would always be on top of the others. Sure enough, every time a teacher drew out a ticket, it was my name that came to hand first and every week I'd be going home with a new prize. As with many things, in retrospect it seems so simple, but at the time it didn't occur to anyone else that the system could be manipulated in such a way. The expected behavior was for students to be extremely well behaved to maximize their chances of success by collecting a large number of tickets, but by taking advantage of the underlying system I was able to win time and time again.

Winning the prize at school, meeting Mark Cuban, getting a job, working your way up the corporate ladder, buying a Tesla—what all of these have in common is that they are outcomes determined by systems. Systems can be manipulated, and in doing so you can radically increase your prospects of success.

And this is what really lies at the heart of everything: a hacker is not just focused on "doing better"—that is to say, on improving their performance—but is determined to succeed. Furthermore, the hacker recognizes that success is not necessarily predicated on doing better. In fact, the key to success is often not in improved performance but in recognizing that there are alternative paths to your goal. This is the very essence of the hacker mindset.

Systems are created to be consistent and predictable—this is why we use the word *systematic* to describe things that are done in structured, methodical ways. But this also means that, operating within the system, you can never be exceptional, because systems are specifically designed to ensure that everyone is contained within the same parameters. Learning to transcend the systems means breaking free of those parameters and becoming the outlier that flies infinitely ahead of your peers.

I learned how to beat the system of the prize drawing at school, and later on I would take advantage of other, more complicated and higher-stakes systems, leading to one success after another.

And I'm going to teach you how to do just that too.

Chapter 2

THE TWO MINDSETS: HACKER VERSUS SLACKER

"Genius is 1 percent inspiration and 99 percent perspiration." I'm sure we've all heard this sentiment, attributed to a variety of people from Thomas Edison to Albert Einstein (in fact, it was author and lecturer Kate Sanborn who first voiced this concept), many times. The idea is that success mostly comes from hard work, that as long as you keep sweating it out at something, you'll be sure to succeed. It's a creed we've all been taught—that there are two types of people in the world, the hard workers and the slackers, and if you want to succeed in life, you'd better not be a slacker. While I'd endorse that last statement, I'm going to say something that will turn that whole dichotomy upside down: even hard workers can be slackers.

I know it sounds counterintuitive, but the way I see it the world isn't split into slackers and hard workers, but rather into slackers and hackers. These are the two mindsets that everybody falls into, and in this chapter I'll tell you about the precise difference between them.

WHO ARE THE SLACKERS?

Nearly everyone in the world is a slacker, and even those who aren't currently have probably been slackers at some point or another. In a world where there are hackers and slackers, the slackers are those who are stuck in systems—those who, for one reason or another, never manage to distinguish themselves from the masses. They're the ones who just go with the flow instead of disrupting systems and carving out their own paths in life. They are all those people who are stuck in jobs they don't particularly enjoy, who are working because they have to rather than because they really want to; these are the people who truly epitomize the slacker mindset.

But just as there are two kinds of mindsets in the world, there are also two kinds of slackers.

The Slacker in Execution

The first kind of slacker is the type of person who is a slacker in execution. These are the types of people who are always dreaming of the things they could do, but never take action to do those things. They are the dreamers who are sure they can make it one day, but somehow that day never seems to arrive. You could say they suffer from an excess of strategizing. The slacker in execution is the person who is always planning, but never doing.

It may not be just down to complete inactivity, however. Sometimes the slackers in execution do manage to put some of their dreams into practice, but then they fail to capitalize on that action. Sometimes when we start working on putting an idea into action, we realize that things need to change—perhaps the idea turns out not to be quite right, or requires additional work around it to be effective. So often success depends upon continued and insightful execution, and the slacker mindset always gets in the way of this.

One of my earlier entrepreneurial endeavors was making an online deal-aggregation website with some friends. You might have come across such websites—they're the ones that list all the various special offers that can be found online, and they make money by taking a cut of completed transactions every time someone buys something via their sites. It's a pretty simple business model, and a good one if you can get enough traffic going through your site. After we built out the infrastructure of the website itself, the focus was finding the deals and posting them on our site. Even with a team of four people and money coming in from the deals we were posting, we quickly found that we didn't have the persistence to carry on trawling through the web and finding more deals. At the end of the day our website didn't have enough content to generate enough traffic to be sustainable, and it ultimately died.

It pains me to say it, but we were slackers in execution. We had early success, and could have pushed to make it sustainable. For the slacker in execution, doing what's needed to reach success is just too much work.

The Slacker in Strategy

On the other hand, there's the hardworking slacker. The hardworking slacker is the kind of person who is all about execution but has very little strategy supporting their actions. They put in all the effort but lack direction and so end up just going down the same path over and over again. They are those people who work day in and day out at jobs they hate, never stepping back to look at the bigger picture and reflect on why they're doing what they're doing. They work hard, put in the hours, and exhibit that good old-fashioned work ethic, but they don't manage to achieve what they really want. Employers love this kind of slacker, because they put in all the effort for the benefit of the company but they never manage to transform their own lives.

These slackers are always following someone else's script. Even if they imagine they're making their own choices, in reality they're dancing to someone else's tune. It's a bit like playing the Game of Life. Have you ever played that game? It's a board game where each player has a little playing piece in the shape of a car that travels along the path of life, as you make certain decisions along the way. You can choose to get married and have kids, to take this job or that, or get insurance or not. Sometimes the path forks and you can choose to take the high road or the low road, but ultimately all the roads converge and everyone remains on the same path. Playing the Game of Life is a bit like being stuck in the slacker mindset when it comes to strategy. You can make little choices along the way, but ultimately you're stuck going along a path that someone else has predetermined for you. You're not able to step back and ask yourself: *Is this even the path I want to walk?*

How do I know that these people are slackers? It's quite simple: I was one myself. When I was fifteen, I was offered a job by Google. I turned it down, preferring instead a job with the federal government. Why did I make that decision? The Google job would have surely been the more exciting and meteoric career choice. Well, everything is perfectly clear in retrospect, but at the time the government job seemed like the better choice. Most of my family had made careers in the public sector and I'd been brought up to believe that when it came to work, job security trumped everything else. Well, if you're looking for job security, I figured you couldn't get much more secure than working for the federal government. Even at that young age I was following the invisible script created by my family and by society more broadly. I think a lot of kids make similar choices—the school system pushes them toward the "safe options," inculcating them with the idea that the most important thing in life is to have a steady, if mediocre, job.

So there I was, working for years in a job that paid reasonably well, expending all my effort and creativity for the benefit of the federal government, taking my paycheck home every month and remaining a cog in someone else's machine. That was until I had my eureka moment and broke away from the slacker mindset, but I'll talk more about that soon.

The slacker mindset is so pervasive. We all know those kids who showed so much promise at school but then ended up being stuck in mediocre careers. When I was at school, I had a classmate called Peter. He was one of those super smart kids—you know the sort—who frequently read books by Bertrand Russell and Stephen Hawking, and found any excuse to get into debates about human society and the nature of the universe. We were all sure he was going to make something special out of his life. He'd go to an Ivy League university for sure and then probably distinguish himself as a leading thinker. Well, I kind of lost contact with him when I left school, but just a couple of years ago I was catching up with some of my old friends and his name came up.

"Peter," I said. "Whatever happened to him?"

It turns out he's working as a sales rep, driving up and down western California selling business-interruption insurance to small-to-medium-size companies. *Wow*, I thought. *He could have done so much more.* I always thought he was going to set the world on fire, but clearly he'd been trapped by the slacker mindset, just like so many others.

Peter, if you're reading this (I hope you are), this book is for you.

NOT A SLACKER BUT A HACKER

If you want to break free from the system and achieve what you are truly capable of, you have to be a hacker. Hackers don't get stuck in a rut like slackers; they know what they need to do and are able to take action on it. Perhaps most importantly, they are able to identify what their goals are and optimize the fastest paths to achieving them.

Unlike the slackers, they are the inventors of their own destinies—they decide where to go and how to get there. Hackers take control of their lives and make sure that it goes in the direction they want.

There are many characteristics hackers exhibit. These include the curiosity to ask questions and the drive to seek constant improvement. Hackers are not satisfied with maintaining whatever system is presented to them; instead, they are always questioning whether the system is optimal and looking for ways to make it better, or even to transcend it. Hackers are also persistent and self-motivated—they don't simply go with the flow but work things out for themselves. If there's something they don't understand or don't know enough about, they will go out and learn about it. They endeavor to remain one step ahead of others, viewing situations from multiple perspectives, so as to understand the situations more fully than those around them.

Most importantly, perhaps, hackers are unafraid of taking chances. In addition to understanding how things can be improved, they put their knowledge into action, effecting real change. Failing to understand and act keeps you stuck in the slacker mindset.

That's how it was for me. In the late 2000s, I was working for the federal government in Silicon Valley and making a pretty good salary as things go. Meanwhile, so many of my friends and acquaintances were becoming CEOs and launching startups and generally leading pretty exciting careers, while when all was said and done, I was really just another employee, another cog in the machine. I couldn't help but compare myself with them. I was earning a reasonable income, but I wasn't in any kind of position to make a noticeable impact in the world through the work I was doing. What was it that I wasn't doing? I had a good job and was progressing within it, but in the long term I could see that I wasn't getting where I wanted to be. What were all my friends doing that I wasn't?

At that moment it struck me like a lightning bolt—up until that point I had been a slacker. Yes, I'd been working really hard, putting in all the hours, but I hadn't been looking at the bigger picture. I was a slacker in strategy, and despite my hard work I wasn't making significant progress in my life. As I continued to think more about why I was doing what I was doing, I realized I was starting to apply my knowledge of hacking to my own life. My taking a step back to consider the direction of my life was the start of reverse engineering—analyzing the situation and working out how it could be improved (more on that in chapter five). I resolved from that point on to embody the hacker mindset in my entire life. And that's when I discovered the idea of the pendulum.

THE PENDULUM

One of the most important things to recognize about hackers is how they balance both strategy and execution to achieve what they want. Unlike the hardworking slacker, who spends all of their energy on execution without a clear understanding of what they are doing or why they're doing it, and unlike the dreaming slacker, who spends all of their time planning but never puts any of it into action, the hacker swings from one side to the other, combining the two. I like to think of it as a pendulum, fluidly moving from strategy to execution, back to strategy and back to execution, bringing the two together in a harmonious equilibrium.

It's just like the pendulum in a grandfather clock—what physicists call a "damped driven harmonic oscillator." It's damped because there is resistance in the system, such as friction and air resistance, which slows down the oscillation. It's driven because energy is constantly being put into the system to overcome the resistance, whether that's from hand-wound springs in old-fashioned clocks or from electricity in more modern clocks. It's harmonic because it's perfectly balanced, never remaining on one side longer than the other but maintaining the perfect equilibrium.

This is exactly what it means to be a hacker. There will always be resistance in the system, whether from within yourself or your surroundings. It's very easy to fall into the slacker mindset, to spend all your time planning and strategizing without putting any of it into action or, on the other hand, to grow impatient and dive straight into the action without enough strategy. It will always take effort and drive to maintain the hacker mindset, both for overcoming the resistance and for striking the perfect balance of strategy and execution. The reward of that effort will be finding harmony in planning and action, which will allow you not only to accomplish your goals, but to accomplish them in the fastest and easiest ways possible.

Most of the hypersuccessful people we see in the world create this balance in their lives. Look, for example, at Elon Musk. As a teenager he was designing and selling video games. Had he been trapped by the slacker mindset, he'd probably still be doing that now, either as a slacker in strategy who was just focused on producing one game after another, or as a slacker in execution who would dream of doing greater things but never act on his dreams. In reality he came up with strategies to become a major success and then put them into action, founding X.com, which would later merge with PayPal, SpaceX, and, of course, Tesla, and achieving great heights with all of these endeavors.

Musk swung fluidly from strategy to execution, then back to strategy and back to execution, and the fact that he is now one of the world's most prominent entrepreneurs is a testament to the effectiveness of this strategy.

There are thousands of potential Elons in the world who could, like him, become leaders in their fields. Applying the hacker mindset is the key to turning that potential into reality.

FROM SLACKER TO HACKER

Ultimately, transforming from slacker to hacker is what it's all about. You need to learn how to leave the slacker mindset behind and embrace the hacker approach. Throughout this book I'll share the various principles and approaches of the hacker and how they can be applied to different parts of life. But from the outset you need to work to embody the hacker mindset. You need to have the self-awareness and self-reflection to ask yourself if you're spending too much effort on strategy or too much on execution, and rectify that imbalance if necessary. You should always have that pendulum in your mind, striving for the perfect balance of strategy and execution and thus maintaining the hacker mindset. With that mindset, the possibilities will unfold before you as we travel together through the chapters of this book.

Chapter 3

THE CHARACTERISTICS OF A HACKER

There's this one quote from Picasso that's always stuck with me. To paraphrase, "Every child is an artist. The problem is how to remain an artist once he grows up." The idea that children are born with innate qualities that most lose as they grow up really resonates with me. The reason why became clear to me when I sat down to describe the various characteristics that typify a hacker.

The more and more I thought about these characteristics, the more I realized that they're nearly all characteristics possessed by children in one way or another. Curiosity, courage, determination—all the characteristics that I'll enumerate in this chapter are present in young children. It just goes to show that each one of us is born with the natural instincts to be a hacker, but as we grow up most of us leave them behind. Society trains us to keep our heads down and fit in, to allow ourselves to be trapped in the systems it creates. There is nothing more disruptive to a human-made system than a thinking, questioning individual. That's why the various institutions that make up society, such as schools or workplaces, have to drain us of these characteristics.

Take schools, for example. You'd think the main purpose of schools would be to educate young minds and prepare them for adult life. That would certainly be the main reason for having schools in society. But the reality is that schools aren't judged by how well their children are nurtured and ready for life as adults. They're judged by the number of kids who graduate. The system is set up to encourage schools to focus on teaching kids to pass exams, regardless of how far removed those exams might be from the real world. What results is a whole cohort of people who have been trained to operate within the bounds of systems without really thinking about where the broader value lies.

It's a depressing thought, isn't it? The good news is that if we're all born with hacker characteristics, then we all have the capacity to remember them and embody them once again. That's what this chapter is all about. As I go through the characteristics one by one, I want you to look within yourself and envision yourself manifesting them in your own life. I want you to ask yourself: *How in tune am I with each of these characteristics?* And then: *How in tune with each of them could I be?* As we reach the end of this chapter, you will begin to see that not only can you manifest all these characteristics in your life, but it will also be natural to do so.

So, without further ado, let's get into the hacker characteristics!

CURIOSITY

The first, and probably most obvious, characteristic a hacker must have is curiosity. Hackers are always asking how a system works and, often more importantly, *why* it works. Underlying these questions is an insatiable desire for knowledge—knowledge that can then be used to manipulate systems and that the hacker can use to make sure they are able to rise above the confines of those systems. Moreover, to be always asking questions requires constantly challenging assumptions. Just accepting the way things are is a default state for most people, but the innovators and disruptors, and indeed the hackers, are those who wonder why things can't be different.

It's a playful, mischievous characteristic. As I mentioned, there's an almost childlike nature to many of these characteristics, and curiosity is certainly no exception. As children, we all learn, at one point or another, the almost infinite power of the question "why?" There is no answer to the question that can't be followed up with again asking "why?" I'm sure we've all done it when we were young. Daddy, why are you going out? *Because I need to go to work.* Why? *Because I need to earn money.* Why? *Because we need to have food and shelter and a little pleasure.* Why? *Because that would make us happy.* Why?

And on and on and on. Now, of course, there is a degree to which this questioning can be just a bit of mischief-making, but in the process the child learns more and more, and so becomes more and more powerful. But as we grow up, many of us stop asking questions. Perhaps we imagine we know it all already, or otherwise that if we ask questions, we will expose our ignorance and lose face among our peers. How ironic that the desire to appear knowledgeable actually ends up keeping us in the dark.

This reminds me of the tension between the two hosts of *Myth-Busters*, Adam Savage and Jamie Hyneman. For those of you who haven't seen it, *MythBusters* was a TV show where Adam and Jamie investigated various rumors, myths, and general assumptions held by the public using the scientific method. Of the two of them, Jamie is the one who is the die-hard empiricist, believing almost nothing unless it was proved to him, while Adam relied a little more on his intuition, as nearly all scientists do. I was once watching a video where Adam was recollecting some of his experiences with Jamie, and Adam told this story where they needed some netting for one of their experiments and Jamie suggested they order some black netting. Adam worried that they wouldn't be able to see black netting properly in the experiment and suggested they get white netting instead, explaining that white would reflect more photons than black. Jamie was skeptical, and as Adam recollects: "Jamie gave me this look that I had had so many times from him, which is like, 'Well, if you say so.'" Adam was understandably frustrated at Jamie's refusal to accept this concept without first having had direct proof of it, but at the same time reflected that it was Jamie's never-ending curiosity and lack of assumptions that made him such an outstanding engineer.

Of course, incessant questioning like Jamie's is not often sustainable in the real world. The difference between a child and a hacker is that the hacker knows when to temper their curiosity with trust when the situation requires. Sometimes in life it's not possible to question *everything*, and in such cases we often have to just go with the flow. At the same time, however, it's necessary to maintain that curiosity to some degree and not make assumptions. It's a bit of a balancing act. Remember that pendulum I talked about in the previous chapter that distinguishes the hacker from the slacker? Maintaining the balance is just like that, knowing the right degree to be inquisitive and to be accepting. This balance is summed up by an old Russian proverb: Trust, but verify.

CONSTANT IMPROVEMENT

Constant improvement is one of the most powerful characteristics I'm going to talk about in this chapter. Most people see improvement as a means to an end. They endeavor to improve a certain ability to a certain degree so that they can achieve something, and once they've achieved it, they stop. For the hacker, however, there is no limit. Improvement is constant and without end, and in being constant it also becomes exponential.

The difference between regular improvement and the hacker-level drive for constant improvement is strikingly underlined in this ironic example. When coding computer programs, most programmers just want to get their code to work. Code can often be quite finicky and will frequently refuse to work if the slightest thing is out of place. In the 2022 yearly Stack Overflow developer survey, over 50 percent of responders stated they spent an hour or more daily searching for answers and solutions, trying to find out why the code they've written doesn't work and how to fix it. There are plenty of online resources where programmers can come together and ask each other about the problems they're facing, and this can of course be a great help to anyone struggling with their code. But remember, most programmers just want to get their code to work, so they might just post the problematic bit of their code and wait for someone to suggest a fix. Once a bit of alternative code is suggested, they'll probably just copy it and paste it into their program, and if it works, it works. Fantastic. There's no need to understand why it works and why the code they'd previously written didn't—the only objective is to get the code to work. The irony is that there have been cases where hackers have suggested solutions to such coding problems that will get the code to work as the programmer wanted, but will also introduce vulnerabilities that the hacker can later take advantage of. The hacker's drive for constant improvement means that they won't be satisfied with something merely working—they'll want to understand the reasons behind it, and in doing so will be able to take advantage of those who are satisfied with things working even if they don't understand why.

And improvement upon improvement can compound. I'm sure many of us learned about compound interest in math class at school: as the percentage of interest is paid into an account (or added to a debt), the amount of the next stage of interest is higher, because it's the same percentage of a larger sum. But the same compounding effect can be applied to anything. In his book *Atomic Habits*, James Clear looked at the compounding effect that would result if you were determined to improve a certain ability by 1 percent every day. A 1 percent improvement each day sounds pretty achievable, doesn't it? And by doing this every day it soon builds up. By the end of a year, just by improving 1 percent every day, your total level of improvement will be nearly 3,700 percent—that is to say, you'll be nearly thirty-seven times better than you were a year ago.

To take a more concrete example, let's say you're doing some weight training at the gym and you find you're able to do twenty reps with a particular weight set. With the characteristic of constant improvement, you might determine to improve by 5 percent every week—5 percent of 20 is 1, so that means only adding one rep in your second week. But as the weeks go by, the number of additional reps you'll be doing will increase. Of course, the number of reps you'll be able to do will eventually plateau—no one is capable of an infinite amount of weight lifting—but at least in those early stages you'll be able to achieve very rapid improvement thanks to the compounding effect.

In the world of computer hacking, this drive to constantly improve has become a necessity. Technology is always improving at an exponential rate, a phenomenon that is described by Moore's law, which more or less states that the power of new computer systems doubles every two years. It's easy enough to observe—take a look at the original iPhone. Back in 2007, it was cutting-edge technology, an absolute revolution in telecommunication. But if you try to use one of those original iPhones now, you'll find it slow, clunky, and utterly outdated. Technology has moved on so far since then.

And as technology improves, so must the hackers, since not keeping up is essentially the same as falling behind. It's a bit like just keeping money saved in your regular bank account. If it's just sitting there and not earning any interest, the actual amount of money doesn't change but its real-world value will decrease as, in the longer term, inflation pushes up prices. It's the same with hacking skills and technical know-how, which is what drives hackers to continuously improve. In the computer hacking community there are events called Capture the Flag exercises: computer systems are created with "flags" hidden inside, and hackers are challenged to break into the systems and capture those flags. There is no extrinsic point to it, apart from the competition, the challenge, and, of course, the potential for improvement. As the hackers put their skills into action, they also train themselves and hone their abilities, becoming sharper and more capable hackers, making sure they keep up to speed with the relentless advance of technology.

Of course, an axiom of the hacker mindset is that these characteristics are not limited to the world of cybersecurity but can be applied to every aspect of life. Whether it's training at the gym, increasing your knowledge in a certain field, or even improving your abilities in a video game, the drive to constantly improve can reliably produce results time after time after time.

COURAGE

When it comes to achieving anything new, courage is an essential characteristic. The one thing that holds us back from trying to do new things, or trying to do things in a new way, is fear of failure, and overcoming this fear is the key to progressing. It's true that sometimes when you try out something new, things will go wrong or not pan out as you'd expect, but 999 times out of 1,000 the risk of this is negligible compared with the risk of not trying in the first place. This is what makes courage such a key characteristic for hackers.

Computer programmers learn this very early on: computer programs are often very large and complex matrices of code, and one slight change in the code in one place can have unexpected effects all over the place. Nevertheless, the programmers *have* to make changes to their code—otherwise, they'll never develop anything new—and so the risk of unexpected consequences is one that they have to accept. Changes can actually be made quite quickly, and the consequences of those changes are also seen quickly, the cycle of making changes and fixing the resultant problems becoming a normal part of the process. This cycle helps computer programmers develop that characteristic courage, and what they discover is that it's not so bad at all, and the benefits of developing something new far outstrip the inconvenience of having to address any issues that arise.

For computer hackers, courage is a particularly pertinent characteristic. It's the job of ethical hackers to break down the defenses of their clients' systems in order to show where the flaws are and how they can be mitigated, thereby improving the overall security of the system. Unfortunately, this often means being the bearer of bad news—flaws in the system's security will usually mean delays in the company's operations, and that's always going to be costly. Of course, ultimately, it benefits the company, as they end up with a more robust system, but regardless of that, company executives are rarely happy to hear that they're going to be facing costly and previously unexpected problems in the short term. If an ethical hacker is going to be effective, they have to have the courage to have those difficult conversations with clients, being the bearer of bad news in the short term, but working toward greater effectiveness in the long term. As with computer programmers more broadly, this is something that trains hackers to be courageous, and having built up that courage, they're able to make use of it in all kinds of situations, which of course they do.

Courage is a characteristic that can be found in the most successful people in all fields, whether that be cybersecurity, business, sports, or anything else. Look at skateboarding, for example. Whenever skateboarders attempt tricks, they know there's a chance that they're going to fall and hurt themselves. But they take that risk, and sometimes they do fall and get injured, but it's only those who have the courage to face those risks and keep on going who become the future Tony Hawks of this world. That ability to stand up to your fears and persist in the face of adversity is so important in achieving success. You're always going to come up against daunting obstacles in the journey to achieving your dreams; what makes the difference when it comes to fulfilling your dreams is the courage to look those obstacles in the eye and push past them. At the end of the day, the biggest risk you can take is not taking any risks at all.

DETERMINATION

As we'll see in chapter four, a principle of the hacker mindset is being offense-minded. A feature of being on offense is that you have to be successful only once to achieve what you want, whereas being on the defensive means that you have to be right on everything. If a hacker wants to break into a computer system, in the grand scheme of things it doesn't really matter how they do it. They might try to manipulate one quirk of the underlying system, or else take advantage of a certain vulnerability, and try and try and try until they're in. And once they're in, they're in. This is what makes determination such an important characteristic. If one thing doesn't work, you can try another—eventually you'll hit upon the solution and you'll achieve your objective.

The cybersecurity company Offensive Security, more commonly known as Offsec, has a certification called the Offensive Security Certified Professional (OSCP), which is known to be an industry standard. If you have an Offsec certificate, you're going to get hired. They became infamous because whenever anyone would take the tests for their certification, get stuck in one of the labs, or fail, they would say, "Try harder." That phrase is so ingrained in hacking culture that someone released a reggae track called "Try Harder." (I'm not joking—you can find it on YouTube!) The philosophy that phrase underpins is that those who failed were not determined enough and if they want to succeed all they need to do is, well, try harder. As long as they're determined, there's no reason for them not to make it.

It's the same with entrepreneurship. Many of the most famous and successful entrepreneurs made multiple (and unsuccessful) business attempts before they hit on that one thing that made them big. Of course, we hardly ever hear about those failed businesses, because when all is said and done their determination paid off and what they are remembered for is their success.

However, we have to recognize that the level of determination must be proportional to the intended goal. Coming back to cybersecurity, let's compare two types of security testing—"pentesting" and "red teaming." Pentesting—short for "penetration testing"—is the process whereby a group of ethical hackers attempts to break into a computer system, figure out its vulnerabilities, and report these back to the developers of the system. The process usually takes a couple of weeks, so for the hackers it's a question of working out the best way to break into the system in that time. Red teaming takes this process further. Instead of spending a couple of weeks trying to break into the system, red teams will often undertake campaigns that last months or even years. They take the determination to a completely different level. So we might assume that red teaming is just a better test of vulnerabilities than pentesting, right? Well, not really—it depends on what your objective is. Red teams are often hired by government and military bodies that are protecting against state-sponsored hackers, so in those cases they're determined to protect their systems at all costs. But for most commercial systems developers, a red team might be excessive and prohibitively expensive, when a two-week pentest would be just as good for all intents and purposes. In both these cases the stakes determine the level of determination justified.

And as with cybersecurity, so with everything else. All those entrepreneurs who abandoned failing businesses knew to abandon them and start on something new. There would be no point in spending years and years focusing on one project that might yield a modest profit eventually—the final result would not be worth the effort. A key feature of hacker-level determination is knowing when to apply it or not and, importantly, in relation to what, depending on what is realistically going to achieve the results you want. Which brings me to the next characteristic ...

REALISM

Being realistic is such an important characteristic when it comes to attaining success. Even in the embodiment of each of the other characteristics, the hacker must remain realistic, and it is the realism that tempers the excesses of the others. Remember the image of the pendulum that lies at the center of the hacker mindset, balancing strategy with execution. Similarly, the hacker balances curiosity, determination, courage, and all the rest with being realistic.

What this comes down to is that you have to be honest with yourself. It's true that these characteristics, the hacker principles that will follow in subsequent chapters, and indeed this entire book will give you the keys to achieving the success you want, but they won't make you superhuman. In fact, an important part of being realistic is recognizing that as a human being you have limits—that you have strengths in some areas and weaknesses in others. The path to success is paved in an awareness of your strengths and choosing to use them to your best advantage.

Understanding your limits and knowing where your weaknesses lie is key when it comes to attaining the best results. Often people who don't understand this try to do everything themselves and fail. Successful people, on the other hand, usually focus on what they're good at, and for the areas where they're not so strong they employ others who have the requisite abilities. In doing so they ensure that every element is being handled by those best suited to do so, and the final result will be the best it can possibly be.

It's also important to recognize that traveling down the path to success may seem like an exciting prospect, and indeed it *will* be an exciting process, but it will also inevitably involve doing boring drudge work. It's the same with computer hacking. Pentesters and red teams have the exciting tasks of breaking into highly secure computer systems, but their jobs also involve a lot of report writing and client management. A good hacker realizes that in the real world you have to do what is necessary, as well as what you want, in order to be successful.

Often, doing what is necessary means working your way through a long process, and being realistic about what is achievable and in what time span. For instance, it's impossible that a teenager who begins working behind the counter at McDonald's will become the CEO of the company the following week, but it could be the beginning of a longer process that leads there—working up from counterwork to management, from a franchise location to corporate. I say "could be" because the feasibility of this path would also depend on the person in question and whether they have the aptitude and drive to occupy such an executive role.

This all reminds me of the Peter principle, a quaint theory developed by and named after Canadian educator Laurence J. Peter, which states that every employee in a company hierarchy is promoted to one stage above their level of competence. The idea is that if an employee is good at their job, they're promoted, and they keep on being promoted until they reach the job they're no good at, when they stop getting promoted. Lacking the competence to be good at that job, they also lack the insight to know that they're no good at it. Of course, this is relevant here firstly in that going up the company hierarchy is a process of stages, but I think more significantly it underlies the importance of knowing yourself. You have to have the self-awareness to recognize where your competencies lie to avoid getting trapped in the Peter principle paradigm. There's no point setting your heart on being the CEO of a company if your skills and abilities are not suited to that role. Know yourself and play to your strengths; that is the key.

And just as you must know yourself, you must also know your environment. Often the situations you'll find yourself in are not favorable to achieving your goals. You may not have the desired resources available, or there may be certain circumstances that impede your progress. Thinking about how things might go in an ideal world is all very well, but the fact is that in the real world things often don't go the way we want them to, and we need to be realistic about what can be achieved and how it can be achieved.

Whether it's being aware of your environment or being aware of yourself, recognizing the reality of the situation is one of the most important characteristics of a successful hacker.

EFFICIENCY

The final hacker characteristic I want to highlight is the ability to be efficient with one's time and resources. We've all got the same twenty-four hours in a day and usually we can't do everything we want to do in that time, so the question is—how do we make use of that time?

Recall that pentests usually last for a couple of weeks or so. Now obviously it's not realistic to attempt every possible way of breaking into a system in that time, so the hackers have to focus on those paths that are most likely to be used by malignant hackers, and to which the system is most likely vulnerable. In fact, this is already partially done for them—the OWASP (Open Web Application Security Project) Top 10 is a list of the most critical and widespread security vulnerabilities in web applications. By focusing on these first, the pentesters provide maximum value to the system developers while using a minimum of their time and efforts. This is the essence of being a hacker.

The OWASP Top 10 is a reflection in the world of cybersecurity of a principle that is found much more broadly elsewhere; namely, the Pareto principle, also known as the power principle or power law. This principle states that in many cases 80 percent of outcomes result from 20 percent of causes. If we take this a step further, by applying the principle of 80/20 to 80/20 itself, you get 64 percent of outcomes from only 4 percent of causes. For example, if you were to spend twelve hours working on something, 64 percent of your end result, well over half, will be achieved in just under thirty minutes!

Of course, the Pareto principle doesn't guarantee that your initial time spent will be the most efficient of your work stint. This is where hacker-level efficiency comes into play. The key is to discover precisely where the most gains can be achieved from your time and focus your efforts there. Sometimes this will be obvious; other times less so. Of course, you mustn't fall into the trap of spending too long trying to work out where the most efficient use of your time can be made. Remember the pendulum of the hacker mindset—you must swing between strategy and execution. Focus too much on the how and you risk becoming a slacker in execution. As with all of these other characteristics, balance is the key.

Of course, for the pentesters, the OWASP Top 10 is there as a guide for this efficiency. It tells them straightaway where they should be focusing their attention. There are guides in other areas too. For instance, when it comes to health there are a plethora of nutritionists who will tell you precisely what you should be eating for the best results, and in the realm of fitness there are plenty of trainers who will tell you where you should be directing your efforts. No matter what the area is, there are always ways in which you can make yourself more efficient, and when it comes to looking at your life in general, this book will help you achieve that level of efficiency.

COMBINING THE CHARACTERISTICS

Each of these six characteristics of a hacker is powerful in its own right, but their true strength comes when they are brought together. Combining two or more characteristics gives rise to what I like to call a super-characteristic, and there are as many super-characteristics as there are combinations—sixty-three, including the six originals. At this point I'll just give you two examples:

- 🗝 **Courage + Constant Improvement = Self-Motivation**
  Developing true self-motivation requires a combination of courage and constant improvement. The drive for constant improvement is of course a foundational element of self-motivation, but so is courage. A self-motivated person must be driven to seek improvement but must also have the confidence in themselves to pursue it.

- 🗝 **Curiosity + Courage + Constant Improvement = Autodidact**
  An autodidact—that is to say, someone who teaches themselves—relies on both of the characteristics that make up self-motivation, in addition to curiosity. This super-characteristic is one I particularly recognize, because it describes me as a child. When I was at school I was always teaching myself beyond what we were learning in class. When I was in the second grade, for example, in addition to my second-grade books, I also bought third-grade books to read over the summer. I was driven to constantly improve and remain ahead of the game; I had the courage and self-confidence to tackle the more advanced material; and I had the curiosity to want to learn more. These characteristics combined made me into the autodidact who would eventually teach himself to hack computer systems and end up working for the federal government while still in high school.

Of course, these are only two possible combinations of many, many others. Why don't you try combining some of them for yourself and see what super-characteristics you can come up with?

We've explored the key characteristics of a hacker and seen the importance of each of them when it comes to navigating your way to success. We also considered how the characteristics can be combined to create super-characteristics, there being as many of these as there are combinations of the individual characteristics. I want to reemphasize here that all the characteristics are there for us to develop and manifest in our lives. There's no such thing as a person who is *just* courageous or *just* realistic. The characteristics develop from conscious efforts on the part of individuals to embody them. If you want to be a courageous person, it's up to you to decide to take risks and stand up to adversity. If you want to be a realistic person, you're the one who has to decide to take a step back and reanalyze things objectively. And so on for all the other characteristics.

Embodying the hacker characteristics comes down to your own decisions—they are not innate qualities.

Having established the hacker characteristics, we'll now move on to look in more depth at the six hacker principles. Whereas the characteristics are general traits that can be developed and, in being embodied, help hackers on their way to success, the principles are specific ideas and processes that hackers make use of in order to accomplish their goals. In the following chapters we'll dive into each of the principles, examining how they are used by hackers and how they have broader significance for all aspects of your life.

And without further ado, let's jump straight into the first hacker principle.

Part II

THE HACKER PRINCIPLES

Chapter 4

HACKER PRINCIPLE 1: BE ON OFFENSE

If you're not on offense, you're on defense. This is the way it's always been since the beginning of time—whenever you have two forces, two ideas, two elements, or two people paired against each other, one will be attacking and the other will be defending. These conflicts are unavoidable, no matter where you are or what you're doing. There will always be competing interests or competing points of view. The question is, when you're in that situation, are you going to take the defensive stance, or are you going to be on offense?

OFFENSE IS THE BEST FORM OF DEFENSE

Do you remember the point I made about being offense-minded in the previous chapter when we looked at the characteristic of determination? Someone who is on the defensive has to be constantly correct, whereas someone who is on the offensive needs only one win to be successful. They can have a litany of failures in their past but it doesn't matter because once they succeed, they've achieved their objective. It's this very dynamic that makes being on the offensive such a powerful position.

A medieval sword fight is the perfect example. The objective of the fight—the "success criteria," if you like—is for one fighter to defeat the other. Now, if one of the fighters strikes at the other with his sword and the other blocks it, the attacker has failed to achieve his objective. No matter: he strikes again, and again, and again, and each time the defender blocks him. But finally, the attacker makes it through his opponent's defenses, his strike hits home, and the defender is killed. The attacker has won the fight, the end result being exactly the same as it would have been had his very first strike made it through. Throughout the fight, the defender never had a chance to attack—he was too busy defending. Every time he turned away one strike, the attacker followed up with another and he had to block that one too. The attacker never gave him the opportunity to do more than defend, and so from that point on, his fate was sealed.

The same is true in all kinds of situations in the modern world. As we'll see throughout this chapter, if you're the one putting on the pressure and everyone else is just reacting to your actions, then you're the one who is setting the agenda for what's going to happen.

IT'S YOU AGAINST THE WORLD

I've opened this chapter with an example of a literal battle between two people, but the fact is that this principle is much more widely applicable. Being on offense doesn't just apply when you're literally in a fight with someone else. In fact, the biggest and most constant conflict we all find ourselves in is the one with our own environment—you could almost say with the world itself.

We all find ourselves located within the parameters of society and subject to various rules. Of course, there is civil and criminal law, and there will be various rules and regulations if you're working in a company or within a certain sector. But then there are also the unwritten rules of societal norms, things we're simply expected to do or not do, and assumptions about what is achievable and what isn't. When I talk about being on offense, I don't just mean being on offense within the parameters of these rules—I mean being on offense against the system itself. Most people remain on the defensive in this regard. They think about how to achieve their goals, but only while operating within the confines of the rules of their environments. What sets hackers apart is that they will take on the rules themselves.

An image was making its rounds around the internet not too long ago. It shows the entrance to a parking lot that has a barrier where people have to take a ticket before they can enter. The only thing is, on either side of the entrance there's just flat grass with no wall or fence. In the grass you can see the tracks of cars that decided to simply drive around the barrier, rather than go through it in the ordinary way. That image is a perfect symbol of what I mean when I talk about going on offense against the rules themselves—it's about not accepting the way things are simply because that's the way they are done.

Being on offense doesn't always come from meticulous planning, of course. Sometimes the opportunities present themselves unexpectedly, and being offense-minded will mean you're best positioned to seize them. One great example of this comes from the career of Roger Federer. Federer is of course widely regarded as one of the greatest tennis players of all time. By 2016, he had earned himself an outstanding reputation, garnered from decades of top-class performance, but whispers began circulating about his waning abilities. He was beginning to get old for a tennis player and it had been a few years since he'd won any major tournament. Then tragedy struck—while at home preparing a bath for his children, he turned awkwardly and tore the meniscus in his knee. It was a major injury and would require surgery followed by months of recovery in which he could play no tennis.

Commentators assumed that this would mark the end of Federer's career. His abilities were declining anyway, so it would make sense to take the opportunity of being forced out of the game for a time to retire altogether. Federer wasn't one to simply sit back and take that, however, and he came back fighting. He didn't spend his time recovering idly, waiting for his injuries to fully heal; instead, he focused on analyzing his own game and working out how it could be improved. Most notably he was able to recognize that his backhand was the weakest part of his game and it had been that stroke that had cost him the most matches in the past. Armed with this knowledge, it was a simple matter to work on his backhand upon coming out of recovery and then going on to storm the major tournaments of the following year. In 2017, he won the Australian Open and Wimbledon, and he defended his title in the 2018 Australian Open. Rather than disappear from the world of tennis, he propelled himself right back up the leaderboard, flying up from sixteenth in 2016 to second in 2017.

And what lay at the heart of this ascension was Federer's offense-minded approach. Most people would have seen the injury as indication that he should give up, but for Federer it was clear that he had to keep on fighting.

Though Federer demonstrated his offense-mindedness in relation to unexpected circumstances—namely, a sudden injury—other times it's necessary to be a bit more proactive with being on offense. When faced with any system, a hacker will ask: *What rules or barriers are there that, if removed, would make achieving my objective easier?* Once they have identified those, the hacker can proceed to consider how to get around them. And just as in the cases of Federer and the medieval sword fight, the same can be applied to any situation.

When we looked at the characteristics of the hacker, I mentioned that curiosity was quite a mischievous characteristic. If we take that mischievous element and expand it, we'll see how it is a key aspect of being on offense. Being mischievous means thinking outside the parameters, doing what people don't expect you to do or don't want you to do. Often, taking this path will lead to you achieving your ends, not least because nobody else is doing it that way.

A great example of this comes from my days in the computer hacking community. Remember earlier when I talked about how hackers stage Capture the Flag events to ensure that they're always improving their skills? Well, early on in my career I was at such an event. It was a pretty hard one, with dozens of challenges that became increasingly difficult, and yet I raced through them with ease. Within an hour I'd completed all the challenges, and the organizers were scrutinizing me with suspicious eyes. They figured that I was either cheating or an absolute genius, but since they couldn't work out how I was doing it they eventually had to concede that I'd won.

So how did I do it? Much as I'd like to say it was all down to my incomparable genius, the truth is I took a shortcut. I'd brought a camera with me to the event with quite a long lens. My intention had just been to take some pictures of the event, but when they were setting up the Capture the Flag challenges an opportunity presented itself to me. We were separated from the organizers by a distance of twenty feet or so, so they were too far to see but not actually in a different room. Too far to see for the naked eye, of course, but not for a camera with a long lens. So I used my camera to take pictures of their screens as they set up the challenges, which just so happened to have all the solutions on them. Then when it came to doing the challenges, I just had to refer back to the pictures I'd taken earlier. It wasn't how I was supposed to solve the problems, but hacking is all about approaching problems from oblique angles and thinking outside the box, and when all was said and done, I'd won the challenges.

And, of course, this type of thinking isn't limited to computer hacking. Some years ago, I managed to visit the Playboy Mansion. Lucky me, right? Well, actually, luck didn't have that much to do with it. The trip to the Playboy Mansion was the prize for acing a quiz at a conference I was attending, and I noticed that there wasn't an official rule that you couldn't look up the answers to the quiz on the internet. I guess they thought it was obvious, but at the end of the quiz I was the only one who had 100 percent of the answers right—everyone else abided by this "unwritten rule." There was a little grumbling from various participants but, in the end, I was the one who won the prize.

I guess this sounds a bit like cheating, but really it's all about being on offense, and it's a great example of this principle in action. Hackers operate outside the normal bounds of societal expectations. After all, hacking is all about overcoming systems and often achieving your goals through unexpected routes. As such, hackers recognize that if the rules are not defined, it's up to the individual to determine what the rules are and how they should be applied. This is often the fundamental principle at play when it comes to brain teasers; for example, where you're given a puzzle and the solution lies in realizing that rules you'd assumed were in place have not actually been stated and so needn't be followed. Recognizing when this applies in real-life scenarios is a key part of applying the hacker mindset. It's all about recognizing that the beliefs or assumptions that limit you need not be followed. Once you recognize this, you'll begin to see that everything is hackable.

GETTING OUT OF THE DEFENSIVE MINDSET

I hope you're not getting the impression that I'm saying defense in general is not important. It's very important. You can't just leave yourself wide open to attack—if you do, it's only a matter of time until someone takes advantage of your weak defenses. But what I want you to take away from this is that by stepping out of that defense-only mindset and taking the approach of being on the attack, you can often make your defenses even stronger than if you'd focused only on defense. We see this exemplified in soccer games, where some teams opt to play defensively or go for a draw, particularly if they don't need an individual win to come out on top in the tournament. Soccer commentators sometimes call this "negative play" and it's generally not very well thought of—it often invites the opposing team to break through the defenses and pull ahead. However, if a team in the exact same situation were to be on offense, playing positively, they'd make it even more difficult for the opposing team to win, as they'd need to surmount an even larger goal difference to come out on top.

Sticking with sports, you often see the contrast between offense and defense in some individual players. There are some quarterbacks who play defensively, just doing enough to justify their salaries but not doing very much to propel themselves into the top tier. We often see the same thing with employees, where there are those who are just doing what's required to take home their pay and aren't engaged in pushing forward in their careers. That's in contrast with the driven employees who are always proactive in looking for ways in which to progress, and they're the ones who end up being more successful.

The defensive mindset is of course found all over the place. I think a quick look at the world of cybersecurity will help us unpack this concept a little bit further. In the previous chapter we talked about pentesting and red teaming. To recap, these are engagements whereby teams of ethical hackers test the security of computer systems by attempting to break into them. They're also a good example of the contrast between defensive-mindedness and being on offense.

Corporations are usually on the defensive. They're not hackers, after all, and their main concern is ensuring that their own computer systems are secure, as opposed to breaking into other systems. Meanwhile, the black-hat hackers are constantly on offense, looking for any way in which they can hack into the system. This puts the ethical hackers in a bit of a dilemma—in order to do their job properly they need to use all the techniques of hacking to test the security of their client's computer systems, but the client will often put limitations on them to minimize their exposure. They might say something like, *Only attack the system between 2 AM and 3 AM*, or *Don't attack this particular part of the system because there's sensitive information behind it.* Of course, black-hat hackers have no such limitations.

One person who frequently came up against this conflict was Samuel Varnado. In the '90s, Varnado was a very prominent figure in the world of cybersecurity and was particularly renowned for his expertise when it came to the security of supervisory control and data acquisition systems, or SCADA systems for short. These are computer systems put into place that allow people to control machine and infrastructure processes remotely, and so are a natural target for malicious hackers. Break into a SCADA system and you basically have a building at your mercy, from door access to ventilation systems. As the '90s went on, the risk from hackers to such systems became increasingly prominent, and though Varnado would warn his clients about them he'd often be rebuffed. It was still the relatively early days of the internet and the CEOs he'd speak with couldn't understand that anyone would be a threat to their infrastructure unless they were literally standing outside with weapons. The computer systems were password protected, after all.

Varnado figured that experience was the best teacher and so he went about showing his clients how easy it would be to bring down their security systems by hacking into them. By the late '90s he'd broken into dozens of the most secure systems owned by a variety of the most prominent private-sector and government bodies in the country, revealing the substantial gaps in their security. The shamefaced CEOs who had previously dismissed Varnado's warnings learned a valuable lesson and took the cue to take cybersecurity more seriously, ensuring that their computer systems were as secure as possible.

I'd love to say that from then on security personnel would appreciate the full importance of cybersecurity, but unfortunately it seems that people still have something of a blind spot for securing the intangible realm of computer systems. Years after Varnado's campaign for greater cybersecurity, I came up against the exact same problem while working as an ethical hacker myself.

I was asked to test the electronic access system of a highly secure building. The physical security team on the ground was pretty confident in the impenetrability of the building, mainly because the guards on duty were armed, and, after all, who's going to get by a guy with a gun? Well, it was my job to show the flaws in their system. After a little work on their digital security system, I managed to break into the network shared by all the electronic doors in the building and brought it down. Now, the system was designed so that if the network went down all the doors, including emergency exit doors, would default to being unlocked. It makes sense. If there were an emergency that brought the doors' network down, you wouldn't want people to be trapped in rooms with no way out—that could cost lives. So, with a little computer hacking I'd managed to change the state of nearly all the doors in the building. The security guards' control panel showed all doors unlocked, though they had no idea how it had happened, and despite all being armed, they didn't have enough numbers to cover every single open door. It was absolute havoc as the security team scrambled to try to secure physical access in the building.

You won't be surprised to hear that the chief of security wasn't impressed with the situation. "Are you telling me," he asked through gritted teeth, "that all the doors in the building were unlocked?"

"Yep," I said, trying to hold back my excitement about a successful hack.

"And anyone—*anyone*—could open the door and just walk in as they please?"

"Yep," I said again. He wasn't impressed. In fact, he began to yell at me. *What the hell was I thinking? Didn't I realize how irresponsible I'd been?* He went on for quite a while and I ended up reminding him that I'd spent the prior night going from one door panel to another, manually reprogramming them so that they'd work properly again so that the impact window was minor. Once he'd calmed down (as the door network was well back in place), the chief of security took me aside and thanked me. I'd uncovered a serious security risk in what they had previously thought to be an impenetrable system.

Being on offense was key to uncovering these flaws. Black-hat hackers would be trying to do exactly what I did, and they wouldn't have had the courtesy to go around reprogramming the doors afterward. Bringing that offense-minded approach allowed me to show the security team exactly where their vulnerabilities lay and now the building's defenses are stronger for it.

Despite all these examples, however, corporations and people in general continue to have a defensive and reactive mindset, trusting in the systems they have in place, trusting in the money they invested to solve their vulnerability problems, and not envisioning the ways in which people could still take advantage of them. Which means, of course, they are ripe to be taken advantage of.

Take the process of boarding an airplane as an example. I'm sure we're all familiar with the experience of hanging about the gate as the passengers are boarded by groups, occasionally glancing down to where it says "Group 9" on our tickets, and just generally hovering around until our group is called. The airline staff rely on the fact that the group is printed on the ticket to ensure people board in the correct order, so if you're printing your boarding pass at home, a little artwork change can turn that "Group 9" to a "Group 1," and then all of a sudden you're one of the first people to board the plane. The same principle can be applied to conferences and expo events, where different-colored name tags give you different levels of access. It doesn't require that much skill with computer graphics to change that color, and if you can't do it yourself you almost certainly know someone who can.

In all these cases the organizations in charge are leaving gaps to be taken advantage of, because they trust in the systems they've put in place. Remember how in the previous chapter I recalled the mantra "trust, but verify"? Being on offense often means taking advantage of the fact that people trust, but fail to verify.

BEING ON OFFENSE VERSUS BEING OFFENSIVE

Up to this point I've painted a very aggressive image of a hacker's approach to problems, which is all well and good, but I don't want you to go away with the idea that it's therefore necessary to be combative all the time in order to achieve what you want. In fact, it's often the case that being supportive and collaborative will be part of the path to success, and this is also part of the principle of being on offense. Let's look at a couple of examples.

In the workplace you're usually in a competitive environment. Not everyone gets a promotion and not everyone gets a pay raise. Like it or not, as an employee you're going to be competing against your colleagues. However, if you charge in there looking for any opportunity to take down those around you, you're likely to get nowhere fast. That's not what being on offense means. You're much more likely to be successful if you're assertive and affable, engaging with your colleagues while also establishing yourself as indispensable. When a problem arises you don't go to your manager saying, "This is a problem; what should we do?" You go to your manager saying, "This is a problem, and this is the solution." And if you're looking for a pay raise or promotion, you're not going to achieve either if you aggressively tell your managers that you're superior and deserve more. In fact, the offense-minded approach comes in asking for the pay raise or promotion in the first place and then showing how that will add value not just for yourself but also for the company.

Similarly, in business you're not going to do well if you take a combative approach to potential clients or investors. Rather, being on offense means getting out there and working toward winning clients and expanding the business. Sometimes would-be entrepreneurs establish their businesses, get going in a small way, and then wait for VC funds or angel investors to turn up and pave the path to expansion for them. They figure they've got a great concept and it'll only be a matter of time before investors start knocking on their doors. More often than not, they wait in vain. The offense-minded business owners go out themselves, showing the value of their business as they pitch for investment, and they're the ones who win it. They'll take a proactive approach to finding new clients—perhaps they'll offer potential clients a little free business to get them interested, therefore generating more paying work down the line. It's all about going out there and doing what's needed to ensure that you're successful, because opportunity is not just going to come to you.

That's how it was for me. When I came up with the idea for Hacker Warehouse, I didn't say: "That's a really good idea; I'll wait for someone to do it and then make use of it." I recognized that this was something nobody had done before, that sought-after gap in the market, and I decided that I was going to be the one to fill it. I took the initiative to form the business, was proactive in doing what I needed to do to grow it, and that offense-minded approach paid dividends in rewarding me with a successful business.

Being on offense as opposed to being offensive is often a key part of innovation in business as well. A great example of this is the case of Steve Jobs. In the early 2000s, music piracy was rampant, resulting from a combination of a huge increase in the availability of the internet along with the convenience of MP3s. Millions of consumers were turning to such platforms as Napster, LimeWire, and Kazaa to download thousands upon thousands of music tracks completely free, and of course completely illegally. The head honchos of the music industry took a reactive and offensive, but crucially not offense-minded, approach to this problem—they went on a campaign of attack, aggressively suing both file-sharing platforms and individual downloaders in an attempt to stop the practice of downloading MP3s. Needless to say, their efforts were in vain. No sooner had they shut down one platform than another one popped up, and the sheer number of consumers downloading music made going after them all an impossibility.

It was Steve Jobs, with his offense-minded and not offensive approach, who came up with the solution. He recognized that the reason millions of people were downloading music illegally online wasn't because they were all hardened criminals with no regard for the law, but rather because that had become the most convenient way to consume music. Portable MP3 players were becoming increasingly popular (Jobs would have known this better than most—the original iPod came out in 2001), but at that point the only legal way to get music onto your MP3 player was to buy the CD, put it into your computer, rip the tracks onto the computer, convert them to MP3s, and then transfer them to the player. In short, it was a massive pain in the ass. Alternatively, consumers could just download the tracks from the internet and put them straight onto their devices.

The solution seems blindingly obvious in hindsight, but at the time it took an innovative and "on offense" mindset to disrupt the norms of the music industry. Rather than label all those people who were downloading music online as criminals, Steve Jobs resolved to give them a platform that would allow them to download music conveniently and legitimately, and so in 2003 the iTunes Music Store was born. The rest is of course history—since then, digital distribution of music, whether through downloads or streaming services such as Spotify, has become the norm, and the music industry was changed forever.

All of this can be summed up in an ancient Latin proverb that I've always been fond of: *fortis fortuna adiuvat*—"fortune favors the bold." Simply waiting for fortune to smile on you is not a good strategy for success; the successful go out there and make their own luck.

OFFENSE IN THE FACE OF ATTACK

In many ways the time to bear the principle of being on offense most is when you're under attack. In such circumstances our instincts tell us to be on the defensive, but usually this is a great opportunity to achieve a win by maintaining your offensive approach. A great example of this is in sports. Think of a game of basketball—the opposing team is at your end of the court, relentlessly trying to shoot at your hoop while your players are doing everything they can to block them. It's nearly all you can do to stop them from scoring. But all it takes is a few proactive moves on your team's part and all of a sudden the ball's at the other end of the court and all the opposing players aren't there because they were on the attack only a few seconds before. The counterattack is often the best path to victory, and it comes from maintaining an offensive mindset even when your instincts tell you it's time to buckle down and be on defense.

The efficacy of offense in the face of attack can sometimes be truly staggering. In 2017 the Lazarus Group, a North Korean state-sponsored hacker group, launched a world-shaking ransomware attack known as WannaCry that brought some of the biggest companies and institutions around the globe to a standstill. The attack made international news as one of the largest and most devastating cybersecurity events in history. Everyone was reacting, trying to work out how to defend themselves from the attack. Everyone, that is, apart from Marcus Hutchins.

Hutchins was a young computer hacker living in a sleepy town on the south coast of England, and when WannaCry made international news he was naturally interested. Rather than thinking about how computer systems could defend themselves from that ransomware, he looked at the virus itself. Deconstructing it, he noticed an odd part of the WannaCry code that pointed to a peculiar web address. Before the virus would infect a system it would try to visit that website, and if it found the website, it would stop, and if it didn't, it would kick in and infect the computer. Naturally Hutchins thought it would be a good idea to check who owned the website, which would bring him a step closer to discovering who was behind the attack. As it turned out, however, no one owned the website—the web address itself was unregistered. So he went ahead and registered the web address himself. It cost him less than $5 and the results were huge. From then on, every time the virus went to check the web address it found the website up and running and so the virus would stop. The ransomware would not kick in and the virus did not spread. Hutchins had effectively brought WannaCry to a halt, and it was by taking on the virus itself, rather than thinking about how systems might defend against it, that he achieved this.

Of course, the principle of being offense-minded in the face of attack applies well beyond the world of computer hacking. In a business context, think of an economic downturn. There's less money moving about, people are spending less, businesses across the board are suffering and losing revenue. You, a business owner, are faced with the question of how to keep things going in the face of all that economic adversity. So what do you do? You'll probably look for areas in which you can cut spending. Marketing would probably be an obvious choice, as it's not directly related to the business's productivity and feels like a bit of a luxury. In ordinary times you'd like to keep the pressure on your competitors and put your name out there, but faced with rising costs and reduced revenue it's not a luxury you can continue to afford. Right? Wrong! This is in fact one of the first things businesses cut when faced with economic hardship, but in reality that's a time when you want to double down on your marketing. A study that looked at businesses during the recession of the early 1980s found that businesses that maintained aggressive marketing strategies saw their sales increase by over 250 percent in that period in comparison with businesses that cut back on marketing. In short, those who remained on offense during hard times won out, not least because many of their competitors took defensive stances.

Being on offense is a key principle within the hacker mindset and one that always delivers results. Whether it's thinking beyond the rules, taking a proactive approach, or maintaining your offensive stance when faced with adversity, adhering to this principle is a sure-fire part of the path to success.

Chapter 5

HACKER PRINCIPLE 2: REVERSE ENGINEERING

Do you know that scene at the end of the original _Matrix_ film? It's the one where Neo realizes that he's the One and achieves the ability to see the source code for the Matrix. That moment, when he looks around and all he sees is code, is one of the most iconic metaphors for what it is that hackers do. Hackers are always looking at systems and trying to uncover how they work on a fundamental level and how they can be exploited, just as Neo finds he can exploit the parameters of the Matrix once he can see the source code. In this chapter we'll look more deeply into this process of reverse engineering and see how it can be applied in a wide range of circumstances.

TAKE IT APART AND SEE HOW IT WORKS

The drive to understand how things work is an instinct that's as old as the human race. Throughout all of history people have been tinkering with things, whether they be natural phenomena or man-made systems, to discover the fundamental principles that underlie them. It's what has driven our progress as a species, whether that be in the advancement of technology or the development of complex societies. It all sounds like grand stuff, but the fact is that the desire to understand things is something we all have within ourselves. By channeling it into the right avenues you can learn how to come out on top. And the most basic way of understanding how something works is working out what it's made of and how those parts come together.

Of course, in the modern world there are plenty of examples of literal reverse engineering. China, for example, with its idiosyncratic IP laws, has spent years analyzing machines and gadgets developed elsewhere and trying to imitate them. Thirty years ago or so, most of what they were producing amounted to nothing more than cheap, barely functioning knockoffs, but nowadays Chinese-manufactured technology has become exceedingly sophisticated. Not only has the imitated tech become very impressive, but Chinese developers have also begun to lead the production of new and innovative products. By sticking hard to the principle of reverse engineering and taking it to its limits, China is now set to overtake the US as the world's leading economy.

In the corporate world, reverse engineering is also a huge dynamic. Companies are endlessly trying to work out precisely what it is that their competitors are doing, either in order to imitate them or to combat them. Pretty much all computers these days use a graphical user interface, or GUI, to allow users to interact with computer programs using the four elements that have now become ubiquitous among all GUIs—windows, icons, menus, and pointers. Before this the main way in which users would interact with computers was by typing commands into a command prompt. What most people don't know is that this type of GUI was originally developed by Xerox, a company that we don't usually associate with cutting-edge computer technology. However, upon the GUI being released, the way in which it worked was reverse-engineered by the likes of Apple and Microsoft, giving us the Mac and Windows operating systems that we're all familiar with today. A few years later, a fifteen-year-old Michael Dell would receive his first computer, an Apple II, for his birthday. He promptly took it apart to see how it worked and after another few years would eventually go on to launch his own computer company, giving us Dell PCs.

And there are all sorts of companies who go about reverse engineering to try to compete with each other. Take KFC, whose unique blend of eleven herbs and spices is said to be the envy of the fast-food world, and Coca-Cola, which has kept its formula a secret for well over a hundred years. Both companies have inspired an endless number of imitators, all of whom have been doing everything they can to work out precisely what it is that makes KFC or Coca-Cola taste the way it does. The basic idea is straightforward—if someone is successful, copying them is a pretty good way of becoming successful yourself, and more often than not it works.

Reverse engineering is not just about imitation, however. Jane Manchun Wong is someone who has used reverse engineering to great effect, but she's not interested in replicating what others are doing. Instead, she focuses on dissecting the code of newly released programs and apps to discover dormant features that are likely to come to fruition with future updates. In doing so, she's been able to accurately predict developments of such major platforms as Uber, Airbnb, Instagram, Venmo, and many others, publishing these predictions on Twitter months before the companies in question had planned to announce them.

Another example would be how video games are reverse-engineered to the advantage of the gamers. Many systems are often "hacked" so that they can play pirated games while bypassing the system's inbuilt anti-piracy protections. I hasten to add, of course, that playing pirated games like this is illegal, but it's still a good example of how reverse engineering can be applied. Less illegally, cheat devices such as Game Genie have been successfully developed and sold on the basis of reverse engineering. In these cases, the developers reverse-engineer the code of video games and work out exactly what kind of code needs to be applied to give the player abilities not intended by the game. The result is a very lucrative product sold on the back of games developed by other companies.

As we can see, no matter what the industry, reverse engineering is, and has always been, a major factor in how people try to get an edge.

PEOPLE, PROCESS, TECHNOLOGY

When looking at systems and considering how best to manipulate them, computer hackers think about them as being composed of various parts. The various parts of a system will almost always fall into one of three categories: people, process, or technology, or PPT for short. Different systems will use these elements in different ways, and to different degrees, but by specifically considering a system through each of these lenses, hackers will gain valuable insight into how the system is vulnerable and can be attacked through any of these channels. And, of course, the same approach can be applied outside the world of computer hacking.

Uber is a great example of how reverse-engineering PPT has worked in business. The people behind Uber looked at the models of taxi services, predominant at the time, and analyzed how they worked. What they found is that they were very heavily skewed toward the people side of PPT and were therefore weak on the process and technology sides. They figured their best chances of success would be to compete with the existing companies on these sides where they were weakest and where it would be consequently easiest to come out on top. So Uber was conceived as a taxi company that focused heavily on technology and process, almost taking the people aspect out of the equation altogether, and they've been hugely popular. Of course, the first consequence is that Uber will end up being weak on the people front—indeed, in the last few years the company has been victim to a number of high-profile legal cases in which the employment status of Uber drivers was put under scrutiny. It makes one wonder whether it's time for someone to come in and reverse-engineer the Uber model, taking on the innovations in technology and process and then outcompeting on the people side.

When it comes to career development, reverse engineering through the lenses of people, process, and technology can be a key path to winning out. Let's say you're applying for a job. Look at it from the hiring manager's point of view. They're going to have a process; namely, going through resumés and cover letters and making a short list of those to offer interviews. They may also employ technology—many companies these days make use of AI systems that analyze resumés for key words and phrases, automatically filtering out the ones that don't meet these criteria. Analyze the technology and processes at play in the hiring method and you'll be able to tailor your application to ensure that your resumé is on the top of the pile of the interview shortlist. And then there is the people aspect, of course. Having secured an interview, you can do your homework when it comes to the person who will be interviewing you. What's their position? What do they do? What do they enjoy? More likely than not, your interviewer will have a LinkedIn page or a profile on the company's website. Do your research and you can come across as remarkably in the know when it comes to the interview itself.

Reverse-engineering PPT is also powerful when hacking your way to success in personal finance. On the technology side, much can be said about fintech and algorithms that analyze market trends, and when it comes to people, there are countless stockbrokers and fund managers who make money from your investing, but not necessarily from your making any profit. But I want to particularly focus on process. Process in the realm of personal finance really comes down to doing the math and taking a systematic approach to your finances. There are so many people—perhaps the majority of people—who earn, spend, and, perhaps haphazardly, save a little. Pete Adeney, also known as Mr. Money Mustache, an early-retirement advocate who managed to retire in his thirties, made this observation. He saw how so many of his peers were just spending the money they earned with no thought of the future. So he sat down and did the math. He looked at various investment options and found that he could reliably make a 5 percent return by investing in very safe index funds and property-rental projects. With that information he ran the numbers and came up with a graph that showed how early he could retire in relation to the proportion of his income he invested. By investing 5 percent of his income, he'd be able to retire in sixty-six years—obviously not a helpful outcome for his goals—and if he invested 95 percent of his income, obviously impossible, he'd be able to retire in under two years. But there were plenty of midpoints, and by investing 50 percent of his income, which was possible by living a more frugal lifestyle, he would be able to retire in seventeen years—that is to say, in his thirties, having come to this conclusion in his early twenties. By reverse-engineering the processes behind finance management, he unlocked the doors to financial freedom.

THROUGH YOUR ADVERSARY'S EYES

A significant part of a cybersecurity operative's role is to look at the systems involved from the perspective of the counterpart. If you're a white-hat hacker, you'll be wanting to think about how a black-hat hacker might be approaching the system in order to block off the attack paths they would go after. On the other hand, black-hat hackers are also thinking about how cybersecurity operatives will have been looking at the system in the hope of uncovering blind spots in its security. Looking at things from your opponents' perspective is always a great way of gaining an edge on them.

Bill Belichick, coach of the New England Patriots, made a name for himself as an expert at this approach. Early in his career he was known for studying tapes of opposing teams, working out the ways they played and developing counterstrategies to beat them. It was a hugely successful approach and was part of what has made him one of the most revered coaches in the NFL. Of course, the availability of football recordings has only increased since he began coaching in the 1980s, and Belichick has continued his approach of studying film right up to this day. In a recent interview he said: "You can really get to everything, between the different angles, the TV copy and so many different ways to look at plays." His ability and persistence in looking at things from his opponents' perspectives is a key part of his coaching prowess.

Another, simpler example of this approach at work comes from my childhood. When I was a kid, I used to play with Magic Snake Puzzles—they were these chains of interconnected segments (hence "snakes") that you could fit together to form cubes. Each puzzle had only one way of coming together to make a cube and the game was figuring out how to do it. The puzzles came in varying difficulties, from easy to hard, and the idea was that you would start on the easy ones and move your way up to harder ones. And that's what I did—I worked out the easy one first and then went on to the tougher puzzles. The higher-difficulty puzzles were definitely more of a challenge. I took a moment to pause and put myself in the shoes of the designers. If I were designing the puzzles, how would I make them more difficult? Well, the player was expected to graduate from the simpler puzzles to the more difficult ones, and it would be natural for them to build on their experience from the easier puzzles and apply that to the harder ones. So, if the designers really wanted to make it difficult, they would anticipate that and make the solution work completely differently from that of the easier puzzles. Working on that principle, I tackled the harder puzzles and solved them quite easily.

With both Bill Belichick and my experience with the Magic Snake Puzzles, the key was to put oneself in the frame of mind of the other side. By working out how others operate, you can come up with the best solution to combating that and coming out on top.

Looking at things through your opponents' eyes becomes emulation when you use those insights to actually imitate them. White-hat hackers do this all the time—they take on the role of malignant hackers, doing exactly what they would do in order to break into a computer system. This is known as "adversary emulation" and is a key part in uncovering vulnerabilities in a system.

In cybersecurity the highest-stakes struggles are usually those that take place between nation-states, and the label "advanced persistent threat," or APT, is often given to some of the most dangerous hacking campaigns that are often (though not always) carried out by state-sponsored hacking groups. APT3, for example, is the name given to a hacking campaign believed to have been carried out by China-backed hackers, with a history of targeting US and Hong Kong victims, and there are other APT campaigns sponsored by countries such as Russia and North Korea. Adversary emulation is a key part of defending against such campaigns. Cybersecurity operatives will analyze every last detail of their attacks, taking the process of the attack apart and re-creating it, until they know exactly how it happened. This means that, in the future, when those groups launch similar attacks, the white-hat hackers will know what to expect and will be best positioned to defend against them.

Of course, the world of business is full of examples of people emulating the competition. It's really not a bad strategy. If there's a business that's doing really well, copying it is quite a good way to become successful yourself. Obviously, you'll need to be careful, as the key to the other businesses' success may not be what it seems to be on the surface. This is where your hacker-level reverse engineering comes into play. The better and more thoroughly you've deconstructed the system, the more likely it is that your emulation will be successful.

PARAMETER TAMPERING

There's no doubt that reverse-engineering the systems you encounter is a great way to make things work for yourself, but one of the most powerful aspects of doing so is when you use your knowledge of the system to take it to unexpected places. This comes down to operating outside the expected parameters and putting the system into what hackers would call an "outer-bound condition." It's about working out how a system functions and then experimenting with the various parameters of that system. The results are often unexpected and frequently fruitful.

A simple example of this would be on an ecommerce website. The website will have prices for various items and the system will have been built to expect every item price to be a positive value. So, what would happen if the system were tricked into believing that the price of one of the items was a negative value? Would it result in the website giving the user credit? Well, it would depend on how sophisticatedly the system had been built, but getting in there and seeing how the system reacts to unexpected circumstances is what parameter tampering is all about. More often than not, this process will lead you to new opportunities to take advantage of.

You'll often also see this approach taken by video game speedrunners, who will take advantage of glitches arising from the player acting in a way the game doesn't expect in order to complete the game more quickly than would normally be possible.

Taking advantage of parameter tampering is not just a feature of computer systems, of course. Let's return to the world of sports and take a quick look at Billy Beane. Billy Beane was a baseball player and coach who decided to reverse-engineer the game to try to get an edge over his opponents. If you're batting, the system the game of baseball is based on is designed to incentivize you to hit the ball as hard and as far as possible. Home runs are there to reward such behavior, so if you hit as many home runs as possible, you'll rack up the maximum number of points. The problem is that hitting a home run is pretty difficult. This is what Billy Beane discovered as he studied the system, and he worked out that he'd be more likely to win games if he just forgot about hitting home runs and focused instead on putting together a team of solid base-hit players. Though there were fewer glorious home runs, the consistency of scoring runs via much more achievable base hits meant that as a team they performed much more strongly than many others. If we analyze this in the context of parameter tampering, we see how Billy Beane was thinking like a hacker. He understood all the rules and parameters of the game of baseball, and then approached the game from an unexpected angle, and that's what made him such a success.

People push the limits of systems in all kinds of contexts. I once heard this great story about cadets in training who were residing at an army barracks. There was a blanket rule that cadets were not allowed to keep alcohol on the premises of the barracks, and since the barracks' perimeters stretched out for miles from where the cadets were actually staying, it essentially meant that they had no access to alcohol, which was of course the point of the rule. However, the barracks was also right up on the coast, and one eagle-eyed cadet noticed that the way in which the perimeter of the barracks was drawn basically followed the coastline, meaning that the sea area right by the barracks was not counted as part of the barracks grounds. So, some of the cadets got a crate of beer and placed it in the sea just off the coast, tying it to a post so it wouldn't drift off, and they had easy access to beer whenever they wanted. The officers couldn't even penalize them for it, because the rule was that they couldn't keep alcohol on the barracks premises, and they weren't. They were still following the letter of the law, but by pushing it into unexpected conditions they could overcome the spirit of the law and do exactly what they wanted.

This is really what parameter tampering is all about—looking for the inputs and outputs of a system, finding the gaps between them, and using them to win out.

MAKE THE SYSTEM WORK FOR YOU

Throughout this chapter I've talked about reverse-engineering systems as a means of overcoming them. The tone has been adversarial, and that's oftentimes the way things are—don't forget Hacker Principle 1: Be on Offense. If you're operating against a system or against people, or if you find yourself in competition with others, a combative approach to reverse engineering is nearly always the best way to go about things.

Reverse engineering will help you recognize when a system can work in your favor and when it needs to be overcome in some way. The key in both cases is to understand how the system works and to remember that you want to achieve your goals as quickly and efficiently as possible. If that's going to involve using your knowledge to supersede the system in some way, then that's what you've got to do, and if the best way to achieve your goals lies in working within the system, that's fine too. The most important thing is achieving your objective, and reverse-engineering the system will equip you with the best tools to do that, whatever your objectives may be.

Chapter 6

HACKER PRINCIPLE 3: LIVING OFF THE LAND

When it comes to computer hacking, there are a few household names. One is of course Anonymous, that group of activist hackers who hide behind Guy Fawkes masks. Another hacker collective that rose to infamy in the last decade or so is the Lazarus Group. I mentioned them in an earlier chapter—they are the state-sponsored hacking group who carry out the bidding of the North Korean regime. In 2014, they launched a huge attack against Sony Pictures over *The Interview*, a Seth Rogen movie that depicted the assassination of Kim Jong Un. The attack included bringing down the company's IT systems and gaining access to some highly confidential and sensitive information that the hackers would eventually release. Sony ended up canceling the film's theatrical release, which prompted President Barack Obama to issue a press release in which he specifically pointed his finger at the North Korean regime as the culprits in this escapade.

So how did President Obama know that it was the North Korean state that was behind the attacks? Well, the short answer is that the FBI told him so. The longer answer is that cybersecurity experts within the FBI recognized elements of code from the Sony attack that were used in previous attacks associated with North Korea. I remember listening to coverage of the event where the presenter, explaining this, said: "Computer hackers are a bit lazy—they don't reinvent the wheel multiple times. If they've got some code that works, they reuse it." Hearing that at the time, I couldn't help but smile—that's *exactly* what hackers are like, and that's what I want to talk about when it comes to the third hacker principle of living off the land. Hackers *never* reinvent the wheel if a perfectly good wheel is already available.

A fundamental quality that hackers have is resourcefulness. Remember, the goal of a hacker is to achieve the maximum possible result with the minimum possible effort (I'll expand on that more specifically in the following chapter, when I talk about risk-based decision-making). When starting a new project, many people instinctively build everything from scratch. It seems to make sense—a new project requires new tools. However, hackers recognize that there can be a lot of wasted effort in this approach. Using what they already have available is the key to ensuring the process is as efficient as possible. After all, if you're putting together some furniture, you don't go out to buy a new screwdriver if you've already got one on hand. Similarly, if you've already developed useful tools in previous projects, you can make use of them again in your future projects.

There is an often-repeated phrase that sums up this attitude: "standing on the shoulders of giants." In ancient Roman mythology, a dwarf who stands on the shoulders of a giant can reach the sky, and this is what hackers do. They make use of all the resources that are available to them, often resources that have been developed by other hackers in the past, and repurpose them for their own ends.

RESOURCES WITHIN THE SYSTEM

Of course, living off the land isn't just about reusing tools you've used before. In fact, hackers often make use of resources that already exist within the system they're attacking. Usually when a computer hacker breaks into a system, they'll want to do something within the system, whether that's obtaining sensitive data, installing additional software, or any number of other things. Whatever it is they want to do, they will need to run some code to achieve their objective. However, many corporate computer systems have end-point detection and anti-virus systems in place that would treat all unfamiliar code as suspicious or malicious and would not allow it to be run. The solution is for the hackers to use the binary code that's already in the system to do what they want to do. That code is already trusted by the system and won't be blocked by the anti-virus software, and so the hackers can make use of it to achieve their objectives. This is what hackers call LOLBAS (Living Off the Land Binaries and Scripts).

This approach sounds a bit esoteric, doesn't it? Let's look at a more solid example of how making use of resources from within the system can reap rewards. At the very beginning of this book I told you the story of how I, along with Kurt Grutzmacher, hacked our way into Macworld 2007. It's a great example of how hacking has served to give me opportunities over the years, but you may have been wondering how exactly I managed to hack the system. The truth is that it was largely down to the principle of living off the land.

The Macworld website used a system of coupon codes to grant users access to different types of passes. You'll have seen those coupon code boxes on most ecommerce websites—usually when you get to the checkout page, there's a box prompting you to put in a coupon code if you have one and, if the code is valid, you will receive a discount or some special perk. More often than not, it's worth putting in a generic code such as 15OFF on the off chance that it's actually valid and gets you a discount. Well, Macworld used the same kind of system. The idea was that if you were a member of the press, Apple would give you a code to enter on the website when you booked your ticket, and instead of being charged nearly $1,700 for the ticket, you'd get it for free.

So far, so good. It's not like the system used obvious codes such as PRESSPASS1, and if a user just tried all possible combinations of letters and numbers one after the other, it wouldn't be long before the website noticed and blocked you—long before you'd hit upon the right code. From a systems' perspective, it seemed like a pretty safe approach. However, as it turned out, there was a flaw that we ended up exploiting, and it basically came down to cutting corners in the processing workflow.

Once a user put a code in, the website had to verify that the code was correct. You might imagine that the code would be sent back to the server, be verified, and then the verification would be sent back to the user's computer. This would be the more prudent method, but in order to reduce the load on the servers, the web developers opted to have the code verified on the user's computer, avoiding all the back-and-forth that would otherwise be required. For this to be possible it was necessary to have the valid codes stored on the webpage's source code so that the site could take the code the user put it and check it there and then.

Of course, we didn't know all of this to begin with, but being the curious hackers that we were, we took a look at the source code of the webpage, and you can imagine our delight when we saw a literal list of valid codes right there. Now, it wasn't *that* straightforward—the codes in the source code were encrypted, but as it turned out it was quite easy to decrypt them, and in a matter of minutes we had the full list of valid codes before us. From there it was a simple process of putting each code in and seeing what kind of pass it offered us. Conference Pass? Super Pass? Nah. We were after the highest level of access, which came with the Platinum Pass. After a few tries of putting in various codes, we found the one that gave us the Platinum Pass and the rest is history.

What lay at the heart of the Macworld hack was seeing what the website itself had to offer and recognizing how it could be used. This is what making use of resources from within the system is all about, and of course this principle is not limited to computer hacking. There are countless cases of how it can be applied to everyday life—let's look at a few of them.

Many people use libraries if they're doing some research and looking for books on a particular subject. This was particularly the case before the internet really took off, in the pre-Wikipedia era. When I was a kid, when we had to do a project for school, our main resource would be the local library. And libraries are great resources, there's no doubt about that, but there's another resource within the library that many people overlook: the librarians. If you're looking for a book on a particular subject, you could peruse the shelves until you find what you want or you could just ask the librarian. More often than not, they'll not only be able to direct you to the relevant books straightaway, but they'll often also give you other useful suggestions too.

Another example would be TSA Cares. If you've ever been through an airport you'll be familiar with the process of passing through security—that whole process is carried out by the Transportation Security Administration, or TSA, and most of us are just resigned to going through it no matter how long it takes or how inconvenient it is. However, what most people don't know is that the TSA has a program called TSA Cares where they provide extra assistance in getting through security to those passengers who are in particular need. Of course, not everyone qualifies for that assistance, but a great number of the people who do are not aware of the program. It's another resource that is freely available and can be made use of.

And finally, let's say you're applying for a job at a particular company and you want to get a better idea of the makeup of the organization. If the company is in the public sector, it will probably have a list of all the personnel on its website, including information on various job titles and salaries. In fact, there are a fair number of private companies that have job details available online also. A little perusing will give you a great picture of what the organization looks like from a people perspective, and you can make use of that information in your job application process.

RESOURCES FROM THE ECOSYSTEM

Of course, living off the land isn't restricted to making use of resources contained within the system you're trying to overcome—there are frequently resources to be found outside the system itself, in the general environment or ecosystem. As I mentioned at the beginning of this chapter, a fundamental aspect of this principle is being resourceful and making use of readily available resources wherever they may be found. In a computer-hacking context, there is a phenomenon that could be considered an extension or subcategory of living off the land; it is known as living off trusted sites. This is where hackers make use of subdomains of very well-known and trusted websites to trick their targets into trusting links that will usually contain malicious content. Hackers can make use of such innocuous platforms as Google Docs and Dropbox, platforms that many people are used to and won't find suspicious and that are easily available and straightforward to make use of.

More broadly, the internet is teeming with freely available resources for anyone to take advantage of. The software development website GitHub, for example, is full of open-source software projects where anyone can come along and use the source code the site makes available. And their resources are not just limited to software development. The "Awesome Lists" on GitHub are user-generated lists that contain and link to resources on all kinds of topics, from the more banal subjects such as video games to more substantial topics such as business and personal finances. And there are many other platforms where resources can be found, usually only a few Google searches away. Let's think back to the example of applying for a job at a company and wanting to get an idea of the personnel makeup of the organization, only this time it's a private company that doesn't have those details available on its website. What do you? If you just straight-up ask for a personnel chart, showing who's on which team and who manages whom, you'll most probably get nothing. But you can do some investigating on LinkedIn and other social media platforms, all of which are freely accessible, and use that information to work out a pretty accurate picture of the business structure. The information is all out there for you to process; you just need to go out and get it.

And sometimes discovering a resource simply comes down to understanding how something we already have can be used. I'm sure you've all encountered ads for VPNs—it sometimes seems like every other YouTube channel has a sponsorship deal with one VPN provider or the other. The benefits of using such a VPN are endlessly repeated in these ads—mask your internet activity and traffic, access region-locked content by fooling websites into thinking you're somewhere you're not. These are benefits using a VPN will afford you, but there are other ways in which you can take advantage of changing your nominal location that are not usually highlighted. One example would be accessing Netflix—I don't just mean getting access to region-locked content, but getting to the subscription itself. The cost of a premium subscription at Netflix is $19.99 a month—that is, it's $19.99 a month in the USA. In Turkey the cost is actually just over $5 a month. If you have a VPN, you can trick the system into thinking you're in Turkey and get access to the much cheaper monthly rate for a subscription.

This is a key aspect of living off the land—recognizing that resources we already have access to and that we may already be using have broader applicability. This could be as simple as making use of easily available resources to hone one's skills by imitating them. This is actually quite common with creative people—many writers start off by writing fan fiction, learning the craft as they go along, and musicians spend a great deal of time covering their favorite songs. Even during the Renaissance some of the most famous artists, such as Michelangelo and Leonardo da Vinci, would often copy the works of other artists, taking the opportunity to learn more and improve their abilities. All of this comes down to taking advantage of whatever resources are available and using them to improve oneself. In the case of the Renaissance artists, this has quite a striking modern parallel. You might have seen a recent surge of AI-generated art. It really is truly astounding—you simply put in a prompt and the program produces some stunningly accurate art. It can do this because it has processed thousands upon thousands of pieces of art, all of which are freely available to view on the internet, and learned how to produce similar pieces. In 2018 a piece of art produced in this way sold at Christie's for more than $400,000.

Coming back to the Lazarus Group for a moment—in 2017 the group shook the world with the WannaCry ransomware attack. Ransomware is a piece of software that essentially acts as cyber extortion, encrypting the data on a computer and refusing to decrypt it unless a ransom is paid. What made the WannaCry attack so extraordinary was that the ransomware was attached to a cryptoworm, a highly infectious computer virus that travels from machine to machine autonomously without the need for humans to open emails or click on dubious links. In the space of a few hours the virus had traveled across more than two hundred countries, infecting hundreds of thousands of computers and affecting major organizations such as Boeing and the British National Health Service. The irony is that the exploits that led to the cryptoworm weren't developed by the Lazarus Group—they were developed in the USA by the NSA. They were eventually stolen and made public by another hacker collective known as the Shadow Brokers, and all the Lazarus Group did was put those exploits together with a fairly typical bit of ransomware. One commentator summed it up as having a "reasonably crude bit of ransomware attached to effectively weapons-grade exploits developed by the NSA, being weaponized and used against countries all over the world."

FINDING RESOURCES EVERYWHERE

Naturally, I'm not suggesting that you go out there to find malicious software that will help you defraud the public, but this story just goes to show how big an impact can be achieved by simply making use of freely available resources. The same is true in completely legitimate enterprises as well. Historically, if you wanted to start a retail business, you'd find it super difficult—you'd need to find premises, invest in payment-process systems, and much, much more. In the modern, post-internet world, it's exponentially easier, and I'm not just talking about building a website for an ecommerce business. There are multiple platforms, from Shopify to Etsy, where all the infrastructure is already in place and all you have to do is take advantage of it to start selling. Does it come at a cost to the business? Sure, but if you consider the amount of time and effort saved, it might just be worth it. If you were starting a business in the '80s or the '90s, it could take you years to get everything set up, whereas nowadays you can have everything ready in a matter of moments, all thanks to the resources that are available.

And these opportunities to take advantage of whatever's available can be found all over the place. Credit card churning is a practice where people sign up for credit cards, make the minimum payment requirements to be eligible for the sign-up bonuses, then cancel the cards. One particularly interesting example comes from the late 2000s when the US Mint wanted to promote the usage of $1 coins over bills, and to this end they instituted a program where they would sell coins to the public with free shipping. What followed was loads of people buying tons and tons of coins with their credit cards, promptly depositing the coins in their bank accounts and using the money to pay off their credit cards. With minimal effort and no overall expenditure (apart from gas to get to the bank), they managed to rack up a huge amount of cash-back, air miles, and other perks afforded to them by the credit card companies for spending money with their cards.

This is quite similar to another story that occurred a few years earlier, and that I still chuckle at every now and again when I think about it. It was the turn of the millennium and internet access for normal households was really starting to take off. Microsoft was keen to take advantage of the surge in internet consumers, so they rolled out a big campaign across the country where they'd give people a $400 rebate if they entered into a multiyear internet contract with Microsoft. The scheme worked out so that you could visit a number of stores, most notably Best Buy, buy a whole load of electronics, and then get $400 off of your purchase on the spot if you signed up to MSN. From Microsoft's perspective it made total sense—yes, they were giving away quite a lot of money in incentives, but the return on that in terms of long-term customers was much larger. However, there was a flaw in the plan.

It so happened that the contracts in California and Oregon were written in such a way that you could sign up for the contract, get your $400 rebate, and then cancel the contract straightaway with no penalties or repercussions. They were basically giving away $400 for free to anyone who wanted. You can imagine the chaos that ensued when word of this spread. Customers thronged to participating stores, eventually waiting in line for hours in order to take advantage of the scheme. I was in California myself and I made sure to get my free $400 worth of goods. I didn't wait hours in line, of course—there comes a point where the time investment is no longer worth the reward—but the loophole was making its rounds on the internet before it became more widely known and I made sure to take advantage of it early on.

When Microsoft became aware of this situation, they obviously made swift moves to close up the loophole, but there was nothing they could do about all the people who had already made use of it. They had abided by the terms of the contract and attained their free goods completely legally. If you really think about it, this Microsoft incident is not so different from how I managed to get into Macworld. In both cases, taking advantage of mistakes made by the designers of the respective systems meant that the systems were basically giving us free resources. This is what lies at the heart of living off the land. In one case it was an actual cyber hack and required a little computer knowledge, and in the other no knowledge of computing or coding was required at all, but both situations exemplify the exact same principle.

And all in all, that's what it means to think like a hacker and apply the principle of living off the land. It's about being aware of all the resources and opportunities that can easily be grasped and making the absolute most out of them, even if using them differently than they were initially intended to be used. Whether it's resources that are part of the system you're trying to overcome or resources that are available more broadly, living off the land is a principle that allows you to minimize your efforts but achieve the maximum possible results.

Chapter 7

HACKER PRINCIPLE 4: RISK

Everything we do in our lives comes with an associated risk, whether they are monumental, life-changing risks or more basic risks such as having wasted a little time. Understanding those risks—knowing when a risk is worth taking and when it isn't—is a key part of a hacker's decision-making process, and as such it forms the fourth principle that makes up the hacker mindset.

EXPECTED VALUE

Expected value is a concept in probability theory that involves calculating the probability distribution of all the various outcomes for a particular event. Without going too far into the math, it's a great way of working out whether or not a risk is worth taking. If, for example, you were flipping a coin and you were trying to predict whether it would come up heads or tails, to calculate the expected value you would assign each outcome a value (say 1 for heads, which would count as a "win," and 0 for tails, which would count as a "loss") and find the average between them, which in this case would be 0.5, to determine the probability of either result. That's quite an easy example, since there are only two equally likely outcomes. If, however, you were rolling a couple of six-sided dice, the distribution of possible outcomes is not even. Two ones and two sixes are the least likely outcomes, because there's only one way of rolling each, whereas the values toward the middle of the range are much more common, with the overall expected value being 7.

Expected value helps in terms of managing risk because it gives you a solid framework to see whether or not your risk is worth it. Let's take the simplest example of flipping a coin, for which we've said the expected value is 0.5. If we add to that the idea of betting on the outcome of the coin flip, the 0.5 expected value suggests that you should bet with nothing less favorable than even odds. Betting with worse odds (say, three to two) will mean you're on the wrong side of the expected value for the coin flip and will likely end up losing out, whereas betting with better odds (say, five to two) means that you're most likely going to end up being ahead. Now, with a single coin flip this probably won't be evident, but the thing about probabilities is that they tend to be borne out with iteration, so if you're betting on one hundred coin flips, you're going to find calculating expected value to be particularly useful.

This approach is a common strategy in the game of poker. To the uninitiated, poker may seem like a game of pure chance. To many casual players, it's all about reading body language and working out who's bluffing and who isn't. Of course, luck and bluffing do come into it, but another big part of playing poker is about calculating risks. You can see the cards in your hands, you can see the cards on the table, and you use that information to calculate the probabilities of your opponents having stronger or weaker hands to make the best bet based on those calculations. In other words, you calculate the optimal expected value in that situation. In fact, former professional poker player Annie Duke has spoken and written much about this concept, and about how thinking in terms of bets can help with decision-making.

Casinos are probably one of the best examples of expected value in action on a large scale. They make sure to calculate the expected value for all their gambling platforms, be it roulette, blackjack, or even simple one-armed bandits. In all these cases the expected value is calculated and the odds offered to consumers are such that, with the iteration of thousands upon thousands of bets taking place, the house will always come out on top. What it comes down to is simple math. The principle can of course be applied more widely, however—we'll see in the next chapter how computer hackers make use of large-scale social-engineering campaigns. These campaigns often have a low likelihood of any one individual being caught out, but so many people are targeted that the likelihood of *anybody* falling into the trap becomes relatively high, and hackers calculate their expected value accordingly. This guides them into determining how much time and energy it's worth putting into the campaign, and in the following section we'll look at that more closely.

Before that, however, I just want to quickly call back to a point I made in the first hacker principle—being on offense—and particularly how offense is the greatest form of defense. We looked at a sword fight as an example, with one fighter constantly attacking and the other not being able to do anything but defend. One thing I didn't mention at the time is that different moves have different values depending on circumstances, with some attacks being more valuable than others. To be successful, the sword fighters need to constantly be evaluating which moves are most valuable at any given point. In short, they'd be calculating expected value in each instance. They'd probably do this unconsciously, but it's not dissimilar to our example of poker players calculating expected value to work out the best move at any given time. Having a mindset where you naturally think about risk-based decisions in terms of expected value is what lies at the heart of this hacker principle.

EFFORT IN, RETURN OUT

The most fundamental dynamic involved in calculating which risks to take is working out the balance between the amount of effort going in with the level of return coming out. For hackers, there's no such thing as working toward something regardless of costs—it always has to be worth the effort. Yes, there are cases where hackers will work as if "money is no object," so to speak (remember what we said about state-sponsored hackers and red teams), but this is only when the stakes are high enough to justify it. No one is going to spend loads of time and money on something unless it's going to result in something of higher value—doing so is antithetical to the hacker mindset.

There are two key factors when it comes to considering "cost": money and time. The former of these is quite straightforward—you can think of it in terms of simple buying and selling. If you buy an item for $100 and sell it for $200, you've done pretty well, but if you buy it for $100 and sell it for $50, that's clearly not a good outcome. Ensuring you're always in the green when it comes to any kind of financial transaction is a pretty obvious way of staying on the right side of risk evaluation.

However, the degree to which time is a factor is not so obviously understood. I think time is often quite undervalued in our society, and as a result it's underrated as a cost, because people are so focused on the easily calculable figures of dollars and cents. A computer hacker won't spend months working to break into a system if it's not going to produce a good return on those months' worth of work. Of course, the value of time applies to everyone and we should all be aware of how much our time is worth. I remember some years ago I had a friend who was obsessed with finding the best deals when it came to getting gas for his car. He'd often drive out of his way to find gas stations that were selling gas at a few cents per gallon less than nearer, more convenient gas stations. It always used to bemuse me. Quite aside from the extra gas he was using to get to those stations, were the relatively small savings worth the half-hour round trip to get to those out-of-the-way gas stations? I think probably not.

RISK AND REWARD

Another element to calculating the amount of effort going in is looking at the amount of risk involved. This is obviously by its nature quite a speculative thing to do, but by thinking things through you can take a systematic and ultimately successful approach. An example of how risk and reward can be balanced in a calculated manner is playing the lottery. Conventional wisdom is that you shouldn't play the lottery at all, because the chances of your winning are so miniscule, but if you sit down and do the math you'll see that that's not always the case. Let's say that the chance of winning the jackpot is 1 in 250 million. In this case, if that jackpot is $250 million, it's such a remote chance of winning you're probably best off not buying a ticket. But if the jackpot is over $250 million, then the return on the $1 ticket is enough to mean that it makes mathematical sense to play the probabilities.

Of course, you're still almost certainly not going to win and you can decide for yourself whether you want to play the game without extreme odds, even if the math is in your favor, but the principle of calculating probabilities on return can be applied across all kinds of areas. In fact, this is the exact principle that venture capital funds work on—most startups end up failing, so investing in them is always going to be a risky business. But by calculating the probabilities of success and ensuring that their return on investment is always going to make up for all the losses, venture capitalists can ensure that they'll always be making a profit overall.

We also need to be aware of the true nature of the risks that we take. So often people overestimate the risks in a given situation, most often when the risks are not monetary and can't be given a numerical value. For example, people are often afraid of failure and hesitate to take risks for fear of failing publicly and being humiliated. After all, no one wants to be known as a failure, right? But the fact is that the public doesn't really care nearly as much as you'd imagine about whether people are failing at what they attempt and in fact tend to forget about any failures very quickly. So many of the most prominent and successful entrepreneurs in the world have had a number of failures before achieving success. Generally speaking, people notice success much more than they do failure. As such, the possibility of failure is frequently overestimated when it comes to calculating risk, simply because the consequences of failure aren't nearly as significant as one might imagine. Adjust your risk calculations accordingly and you'll see that there are actually so many more instances when it makes sense to take action.

Related to the fear of failure is resistance to change. This is another inhibiting factor that leads people to overinflate their calculations of risk. It can be easy to become accustomed to the way things are and find comfort in that. We might think that something works well enough and messing around with it might make things worse. But let's remember the characteristics of the hacker; namely, the characteristic of constant improvement. Hackers are never simply satisfied with the status quo, and the only way to improve things is to change them up. Whether this means changing jobs, trying out a new business strategy, or taking a new approach to your investment portfolio, the simple fact that things will change is not in itself a risk factor. Change is always necessary for things to improve.

Coming back to the notion of time, it's also useful to recognize here that our capacity to take risks often diminishes as we get older. On the one hand this is just due to the fact that as people grow older they naturally become a little more conservative and risk-averse—this is a state of mind and can be overcome. But on the other hand, there are also factors that make taking risks more difficult. As people grow older, they often have more commitments and responsibilities. They might have a mortgage to pay off or have started a family and have children to look after, and these will often mean that the stakes of taking risks are a little higher. This doesn't mean that if you have such responsibilities you shouldn't take risks at all, but it's good to bear in mind, particularly if you're younger and have fewer commitments, that it may not be so easy to take chances in the future.

And just as it's important to calculate the true amount of risk in any given venture, it's also important to calculate the true value of the reward you might get. As with risk, if it's just a question of numbers, it's a straightforward bit of math (remember the example of the lottery ticket). But often there can be additional benefits to attempting something, which you should also factor in. Let's say you're a business owner and you're considering attending a conference to drum up some business. Your primary aim will be to get new clients, but even if you don't get any as a direct result of the conference, you'll still be spreading the word about your business and increasing your prominence in the market. Sometimes the concept of reward may even be removed from yourself. Elon Musk, for example, has been very successful with Tesla and is now pressing forward with SpaceX. Before embarking upon each enterprise, however, he calculated that the chances of either business succeeding were rather low. What spurred him on to pursue both businesses was the idea that, even if they didn't turn out to be personal successes for him, they were important movements for human advancement. Factoring that into the risk-reward balance made it pretty clear that Elon pursuing these enterprises was the right choice.

The balance between risk and reward reminds me of a story from my days as an ethical hacker. There was this bank-to-bank computer system that had been developed to transfer vast sums of money and it was naturally designed with many layers of security, each step involving a number of checks. It was a big, complicated system with many interconnected parts, and though from an engineering perspective it was well understood, no one had really looked at how it all came together from a security perspective. Everyone involved in each part of the system was confident in the security of their own part, and trusted in the security of all the other parts. On the face of it, this made sense—if each stage of the system has good security, then the system as a whole should have good security, right? And after all, the system had been in use for a while and no one had ever managed to hack it. As far as the developers were concerned, the risk of there being a major flaw in the system might as well have been zero. Well, I wasn't going to take that for granted. I took it upon myself to look at the system as a whole from a security perspective.

I spent days just reading the manuals for the system, understanding how the whole process worked, what it should do, what it shouldn't do, how each step related to the next. I then had the system set up for myself so I could tinker around with it and put pressure on the places where I thought there might be gaps. Going through that process, I discovered a vulnerability (commonly called a 0day or zero-day) that no one had known of before, not even the software company that created parts of the system. As it turned out, though all the individual parts of the system had their own levels of security, the process between two layers wasn't as secure as the developers had assumed. From my perspective, I'd put a lot of time and effort into investigating the system's security, on the hunch that there was something to find. The risk that I wouldn't find anything was considerable, but the related reward should my hunch prove to be correct was big enough to make it worthwhile, and of course in this case it paid off.

As long as you continue to calculate the balance between the associated risks and rewards of any venture, you'll be sure to come out on top in the long run.

TO BE AN OPPORTUNIST

Up to this point we've thought about calculating risk in terms of looking at the balance between cost and return for the various options you have before you. But a broader way in which to apply this principle is by going out and looking for that cost-reward balance that suits you best. In other words, it's about setting out to find where the opportunities lie.

This opportunistic approach is something you'll often find hackers taking. It derives from the characteristic of being efficient that I spoke about in chapter three. Remember the story about cybersecurity operatives using the OWASP Top 10 to cover the most widespread and critical web security vulnerabilities? Well, the corollary to that from a black-hat hacking perspective would be scanning the internet looking for vulnerabilities. The internet itself is a mass of intercommunication, with millions of computers sending packets of information to each other. Hackers can easily send out thousands of these information packets like probes, and judging on the information that comes back they can build up an idea of the integrity of the computer systems they come into contact with. It's pretty much an automated process so it's very low cost, and it's low risk as well—the worst that might happen is that you'd find yourself banned from a server, which can easily be circumvented with the use of a VPN. As a result, black-hat hackers will be rewarded with some very useful information about where hacking opportunities lie.

Of course, not all opportunities are equally valuable. For example, about twenty years ago there were practically no corporations that were using Apple Macs in their businesses, so if you were a malevolent hacker who wanted to take advantage of corporations and you'd discovered a vulnerability in Mac operating systems, that particular opportunity wouldn't have been much use to you. The chances are, however, that if you were scanning the internet thoroughly you would come across vulnerabilities in other systems that you could make use of. Hackers are always looking for new opportunities, and crucially they're often not looking for specific vulnerabilities. By taking the broad approach they come across the vulnerabilities they can take advantage of.

Often, when vulnerabilities are discovered, the developers of operating systems will release patches and updates to close off those vulnerabilities. However, not all users will have those patches applied straightaway. One clever approach some hackers take is to analyze the patch that is released and work out what vulnerability the patch was addressing, and then send out attacks across the internet targeting that vulnerability and looking for users who hadn't implemented the patch yet. This was the strategy taken by many hackers in 2014 during the Shellshock incident, where a vulnerability was discovered (and patched) in many Mac and Linux machines that would allow a hacker to execute their own code on the machines remotely. Hackers were literally sweeping the internet, sending out these attacks that would take advantage of the bug, and wherever they found an unpatched system, the attack would take hold and the hacker would have access to another system. This opportunistic approach proved to be very fruitful for the malicious hackers looking to take advantage of such vulnerabilities.

Looking at things from the other side, ethical hackers are aware of this propensity of black-hat hackers to look for opportunities. As I've spoken about previously, it's the job of ethical hackers to think the way black-hat hackers think and use that knowledge to better protect the systems they're working on. They will look at the system and work out what opportunities malevolent hackers would find and make sure to cover them—this is another example of adversary emulation, which we looked at a few chapters ago when we focused on the principle of reverse engineering. This can also be thought of as a second degree of calculating expected value—that is, calculating the expected value of the black-hat hackers, and then using that to recalculate your own risk/reward balance to block off that opportunity.

The key point to take is that employing the hacker mindset to calculate expected value includes always being on the lookout for opportunities, and recognizing that opportunities might not always lie in the areas you would expect. A prime example of this would be how surprisingly underutilized the internet still is in business. Even though we've been using the internet for decades now and we're all very well accustomed to the idea of internet shopping, there are still countless prospective business owners who shun the idea of ecommerce. Perhaps the idea of being the proprietor of a brick-and-mortar store is still very alluring, but the reality is that when it comes to looking for opportunities, the internet is really the place to go. There are just far fewer barriers to entry when it comes to online business. Perhaps you might like the idea of a nice, shiny store on the high street, but if the opportunities are online, then that's where you need to go. That's what it means to be an opportunist.

ASYMMETRIC RISK

As we've seen, the key to working out risk is gauging the balance between effort expended and reward received for a particular enterprise, determining whether that balance is worth it and looking for opportunities where that balance is met. But the highest level of applying this principle is not just in determining whether the effort-reward balance is worth it, but in determining where it's optimal. Balance can be found in a high-risk, high-reward scenario, and in a low-risk, low-reward scenario, but the ideal would be to have a situation where there's low risk and high reward. In other words, where the risk is asymmetric in your favor, you stand to gain a lot and have to give up very little.

Remember the example of buying a lottery ticket, where the jackpot is greater than the cost of entry while factoring the probability of winning? Well, that's a perfectly good way of calculating expected

value, but it's still a high-risk scenario, because your chances of winning are miniscule, even if mathematically it makes sense to buy the
ticket. On the other hand, you could lower your risk by buying millions and millions of lottery tickets, but then the reward would be
substantially lower as well (to say nothing of all the time expendi-
ture). The ideal situation would be to buy a single lottery ticket and
have a good chance of winning the jackpot.

Okay, so that's obviously not going to happen—the point of this
chapter is not to tell you how to buy a winning lottery ticket, but it's
to show that a key to being successful is to make decisions where the
risk is lowest and reward is highest. This is what investors call "finding
alpha." In the world of finance, alpha refers to the ability of an investor to beat the market—that is to say, they make returns on investments that are larger than general growth in the market. Relying on
normal market growth is not a bad strategy by any means—there are
plenty of index funds that garner success on that exact principle—but
those investors who find alpha are the ones who come out ahead of
the rest, because they're striving for that sweet spot where they get
maximum return from minimum investment.

The opportunity to take advantage of asymmetric risk is not just
limited to financial strategies. You might have seen that episode of
Last Week Tonight where John Oliver talks about televangelists. Over
the course of the episode he takes a deep dive into the tax-exempt
status given to churches and other religious organizations, and the
stunningly low bar those organizations have to meet in order to qualify for such status. In typical John Oliver fashion, he finishes up the
episode by founding his own religious organization, Our Lady of Per-
petual Exemption. It's a great piece of television satire, but what he
really highlights is the asymmetric risk that many such organizations
have in meeting such a low bar to achieve a very favorable tax status. Not that I'm saying we should all form ourselves into tax-exempt
churches, but if you did have a business that could be considered

to fall under the IRS's criteria for a religious organization, it'd be a no-brainer to apply for the tax-exempt status.

The fact is, we're all surrounded by asymmetric risks all the time—it's just a question of recognizing it. Remember a few pages ago, I talked about how an important part of calculating was realizing the true value of the risks and rewards involved? Well, if you really think about it, you'll see that we're surrounded by low-risk opportunities. If you want something, often simply asking for it will produce some kind of result, and the risk is minimal. The worst that could happen is that someone says no. Do you want that promotion at work, or a pay raise? Just ask! Entrepreneur Noah Kagan has spoken a lot about being more proactive in overcoming social anxieties and stigmas to achieve the things you want, and he issued the Coffee Challenge. The idea is that every time you order your coffee at Starbucks or any other coffee shop, you should ask for a 10 percent discount. Most of the time they'll probably say no, but sometimes they'll say yes, and it won't have cost you anything. It may seem like a small gain, but realizing how many low-risk opportunities surround us just by asking is a huge strength that will enrich your life. It doesn't even have to be about your career or finances. What about that person you have a crush on? Just ask them out on a date—they might say yes! We've all heard that nice guys come in last, but that's not true; the people who come in last are those who never ask.

Chapter 8

HACKER PRINCIPLE 5: SOCIAL ENGINEERING

In 2020, a group of hackers managed to hijack a number of high-profile Twitter accounts, belonging to the likes of Barack Obama, Bill Gates, Kanye West, and Kim Kardashian to name a few individuals, as well as the accounts of some big companies, such as Apple and Uber. They used their access to these accounts to make posts convincing people to transfer bitcoin to their accounts, promising that the bitcoin would be returned and doubled. They managed to bring in hundreds of thousands of dollars.

But how did they gain access to these accounts? You might assume that they used some obscure and powerful computer hacking programs to break into the Twitter system, the way they do in movies—hackers typing away at computers in a darkened room until someone stands up and announces: "I'm in!" Nothing could be further from the truth, however. The hackers didn't attack Twitter's technological infrastructure at all; instead, they targeted some of Twitter's employees. They tricked a few low-level users into compromising their credentials and from there were able to go after employees with higher access, eventually gaining access to Twitter's mainframe. From there it was a simple matter to grant themselves access to the accounts in question. In a statement after the attack, Twitter confirmed: "The attackers successfully manipulated a small number of employees and used their credentials to access Twitter's internal systems, including getting through our two-factor protections. As of now, we know that they accessed tools only available to our internal support teams."

This is what hackers call social engineering—taking advantage of the people involved in a system in order to manipulate it—and it's a key strategy when it comes to hacking any system.

HUMANS ARE THE WEAKEST LINK

In the reverse engineering chapter we talked about analyzing systems through the lenses of people, process, and technology. Here we're going to focus specifically on the people aspect of PPT.

When it comes to analyzing and manipulating systems, there's one thing that we cannot ignore—the fact that pretty much every system that surrounds us is composed of people or otherwise has people at its core. This brings us to quite an obvious but also a bit of a morally dubious point: that often the best way of taking advantage of a system will involve manipulating the people involved. This can be difficult to accept, so I'd like to take a couple of moments here to reflect on some of the points I made earlier on in this book about ethics. As I said earlier, I'm not here to take a moral position. The abilities and tools that come as a result of applying the hacker mindset can be powerful, and they can be used ethically as well as unethically. It's up to you to take responsibility for how you use them. As you'll see throughout the course of this chapter, taking advantage of people's positions within a system is not the same as being an immoral manipulator—often the reality is quite the reverse.

With that said, let's think about how humans operate. Of course, there's a wide variety of ways in which people behave. Some may act rationally, others may act irrationally, and for most people their behavior is probably a mix of the two. But whether people are acting rationally or irrationally, there will always be patterns to their behavior, and those patterns can be used to your advantage.

All of us act differently, of course, but it is possible to look at people as falling into certain categories. There are loads of ways to do this, many of which you may be familiar with—for example, the Myers-Briggs Type Indicator (MBTI) personality test, the Four Tendencies framework, and the Enneagram test, among many others. What all of these do is allow you to look at people through the lens of certain characteristics, and doing so will help you better understand how best to deal with such individuals. For example, if there's an individual who fits into a category that is always combative, understanding that personality type is going to help in dealing with that combative nature.

And as we get to know people individually, we become familiar with all their little foibles and neuroses. We know we need to interact differently with different people and we do it subconsciously all the time. Thinking like a hacker comes in when you recognize how people fit into systems and use that information to your advantage.

One way of applying this principle is to consider the roles people play within particular systems. Let's think for example about laws and rules. It's people who make the rules, people who interpret the rules, and people who enforce the rules, and, most often, it's different sets of people who are doing each of these. Tax laws are a great example of this. The tax laws are formed by legislators who have particular goals in mind. This means that the laws are often quite complicated and involved, and so there are a whole raft of other people, accountants and tax lawyers, whose job it is to interpret those laws. Then you have the IRS and a whole host of judges who are the ones who enforce the laws. All this is to show that, though the tax code may seem like a rigorous and inflexible system, understanding the roles these people play in that system and taking advantage of their human natures is often key to making it work for you. In fact, one of the abilities that consumers of legal services most frequently appreciate in their lawyers is not just the knowledge of the law, but the ability to judge how the law is going to play in the real world of human players. Similarly, in court the best attorneys are those who can gauge how the judges and juries in question will react to certain arguments, and use the ones that are most likely to persuade those people.

You might be thinking that this all sounds a little rarified—after all, not everyone's a tax lawyer. But in reality opportunities to take advantage of the human elements of contrived systems of rules lie all around us. Another more common example might arise at a time when there's high inflation. At such times, prices of commodities rise so quickly that there's sometimes a discrepancy between the listed price for an item in a store and the actual price it's being sold for in the store's system, simply because they haven't had the chance to change the price label yet. This is a particular issue for some of the bigger retail chains like Target, and it's for this reason that they give the cashiers the power to charge the lower price for an item when such a discrepancy exists. But now get in the head of that cashier. They might just be some kid working at a low wage, not massively invested in the overall success of the store. Inflation is high, so it's not uncommon for customers to complain that the listed price was lower than the price at the register, and in such cases the cashier has been told to charge the lower price. Are they really going to get up and check the price if you say: *Hang on a minute—you just rang me up for $11.99, but the price on the item was $9.99?* Maybe. Maybe not. It's something you'd have to make a judgment on. Store policy is probably that they have to, but remember, the cashier is a human, not a machine, and gauging how the cashier is going to act as a human being would be key in this situation to hacking your way to a discount. Now, this obviously isn't the most ethical thing in the world and I'm certainly not suggesting you go out there and try to deceive cashiers to get a few dollars off your purchases, but this is an example of how human beings working within systems always come with expectations and assumptions, and those are things that you can take advantage of.

PEOPLE ARE (GENERALLY) NICE

One thing that is very easy to forget is just how nice most people are. When you find yourself within a social system, either competing with others or in outright opposition to them, it's quite natural to assume that everyone is going to have an antagonistic disposition toward you. However, the fact is that that's usually not the case. More often than not, people are disposed to be nice, polite, and helpful. They are predisposed to trust you—when two strangers talk to each other, the vast majority of the time they will start from a position of believing the other is speaking the truth. This is particularly true if someone doesn't see you as an adversary, regardless of whether or not you are one. And even if they do see you as adversarial, they're not going to have their guard up all the time. It's human nature to become lax, to drop one's guard, as well as to have the instinct to be trusting and helpful. Put this all together and you'll be in a great position to take advantage of situations involving human interaction.

I've used this many, many times in my career as a hacker. During red team operations we'd often try to gain physical access to allegedly secure buildings, as on-site security goes hand in hand with cybersecurity. It's amazing how far a set of scruffy work clothes and a name badge will get you, or a high-visibility jacket and a clipboard. The propensity for people to trust you and take your appearance at face value goes a long, long way, and if you're dressed as a laborer, nine out of ten security guards will think: *Ah, they've been hired to fix something; I'll just let them in.* I've accessed so many buildings that were supposed to be off limits, all by taking advantage of the human dynamics at play. And it's not just me and my hacker peers—anyone can take advantage of people's expectations in this way. Australian comedian Steve Philp once went out of his way to prove his theory that you could go anywhere with a ladder under your arm. Simply by carrying one, with no other visual identifiers, he was able to get access to a whole variety of places, including the kitchen of a restaurant, the subway, a cinema, and a boat on the river. All by making use of people's assumptions.

As I mentioned, you can take advantage of people's good nature most particularly when they don't see you as an adversary, but even when they do, being cognizant of the social dynamics will pay dividends. If you find yourself on the wrong end of a personal attack, the thing *not* to do is to follow the natural instinct of being defensive (remember Hacker Principle 1: Be on Offense). Rather, remember one of the things we talked about when we looked at the principle of reverse engineering—namely, adversary emulation. The thing to do is to get into their head, to work out what they want, why they're doing what they're doing, and what they're trying to achieve. Understanding what's driving them and what their incentives are will put you in a much stronger position when it comes to dealing with them, whether that's by triumphing over them with a counterattack, or by simply defusing the situation.

PRETEXTING

Pretexting is a common technique used by computer hackers and scammers to try to attain personal or sensitive information. Though these days it's commonly associated with scam artists, it actually has a history that goes all the way back to the 1970s, when the FBI used it to help its investigations. What it essentially comes down to is pretending to be someone you're not in order to get some kind of information or other gain from a target. Surely you're familiar with receiving calls from unknown numbers, from people claiming to be from the IRS or from insurance companies—these are well-known scams, but they are also examples of the social engineering method of pretexting.

There is a broad range of techniques that pretexters use with their targets, ranging from simple persuasion to intricate deception, but the principles are always the same—that is to say, making use of predictable human characteristics to increase the chances of achieving your goal. These characteristics include the common trusting nature that I spoke about earlier; pretexters will often build on this to establish a trustworthy rapport with their targets. They will also make use of the tendency people generally have to react emotionally, particularly when it seems there are high stakes involved. For example, a pretexter might suggest that their target wire a large sum of money or else their savings are at risk of being stolen. In either case the target's instincts will be to react with emotions that would likely override their prudence. And a third technique pretexters might use is the appearance of authority. People generally respect authority and it can be quite straightforward to project an authoritative persona. It can simply come down to speaking with confidence and using an accent and tone of voice associated with the higher classes.

Of course, pretexting is often associated with scammers, but it does have broader applicability. Remember how I spoke a little earlier about gaining access to off-limits areas simply by wearing a high-vis jacket or carrying a ladder? That's also a form of pretexting. The key is that it takes advantage of the fact that people have assumptions and will rely on them. And though scammers often use this technique to take advantage of vulnerable people, at a higher level pretexting can take even some of the savvier targets unawares. One story in particular springs to my mind.

One time one of the members of my cybersecurity team, Matt, was testing the security of the HR department within a company. We embedded some remote access code in the Word documents of a resumé, sent them to the HR department recruiters, and then waited until one of them would bite. The thing is, the code was contained in a subprogram called a macro, and in order for the code to be executed the user would have to enable macros when they opened the document.

One of the recruiters gave us a call back for an initial telephone interview screening. Matt asked them if they had any questions about the resumé, to which the recruiter replied that they hadn't actually been able to open it. They had come across a resumé that prompted them to enable macros and so they were rightly suspicious of it. Matt carried on talking with the recruiter like normal, building up rapport and convincing them that he was just a normal guy like anyone else. The recruiter began to warm up to him, edging closer and closer to trusting him, but never quite getting to the point where they were going to open the resumé. They talked for over an hour about the various aspects of the role, discussed Matt's supposed work history, and even conducted an on-the-spot technical pop quiz. By the end they still hadn't opened the resumé and Matt was just about ready to give up. They said their goodbyes and Matt hung up the phone, feeling defeated. He was sure they weren't going to open the resumé now, and he thought he might have been a bit too obvious and blown the whole operation.

Thirty minutes later he got a notification on his computer that the code in the macro had been executed. Despite how it had seemed, all that work Matt put in convincing the recruiters that he was genuine paid off and they had finally opened the resumé and allowed the code to execute. The recruiter's completely correct level of caution had been overcome by Matt's persistent personableness. This example just goes to show that you can achieve your goal with the right mixture of social engineering tactics, even when you've almost completely given up on it working out.

Though I've been talking a lot about computer hackers and digital scam artists when it comes to pretexting, the techniques themselves have nothing to do with technology—it's all about recognizing common human traits and using them to your advantage. I know this all sounds quite sinister; there's no denying that these techniques are widely employed by scammers and fraudsters, but as usual they can be much more broadly applied. Take that scene from the classic movie *Ferris Bueller's Day Off*, for example, where Cameron calls into the school principal pretending to be Sloane's father to get her out of school for the day. If you haven't seen it, it's well worth a watch, and it's a great example of pretexting in action. Cameron imbues his voice with authority and takes advantage of the principal's social decorum and embarrassment to get what he wants.

LARGE-SCALE SOCIAL ENGINEERING

I'm sure most of you are now familiar with the concept of phishing and its variants, vishing and smishing. For those who are not familiar, phishing involves sending emails to very large numbers of people with the aim of getting some kind of personal information. The emails will often look like the kind of emails many people would expect to receive, such as a notification that an Amazon order is going to be delivered or that a bank transaction has failed, with the aim of getting the recipient to click on a link. The phisher then tries to get some kind of personal information, whether that be passwords or bank account details or anything else. And then from phishing, variants have arisen such as smishing (social engineering via SMS text messages) and vishing (social engineering via calls and voice messages). Of course, most of us are inured to such attacks and can usually spot them without much trouble, but that's where the large scale of the operation comes in. The phishers don't need everyone to fall for their fake emails; they don't even need most to—just a handful will give them what they want and make the whole activity worthwhile.

The important thing to focus on here is the large-scale nature of these attacks. They don't have to succeed with every single attempt—in fact they certainly don't. But the operations are conducted at large-enough scales to ensure that they will be successful a significant number of times. Do you know who else uses this large-scale technique? Marketing campaigners. Does everyone who sees an ad for Hershey's go out to buy a bag of Kisses? No, of course not, but some will, so overall it's worthwhile for Hershey's to run ads. The key point to note here is that sometimes a large-scale approach is the path to ultimate success. In such cases you shouldn't worry about individual instances of failure or be discouraged—the goal is not to succeed at every single instance, but to succeed overall. When we were looking at expected value in the chapter on risk, we saw how probabilistic events can become deterministic with iteration. Recall how casinos will always come out on top because, even though there may be some gamblers who win large amounts, overall the odds are always in the casino's favor. That's exactly the principle at play when it comes to large-scale social engineering. It might be that only a small proportion of your attacks succeed, but as long as the gains from your success are sufficiently high, overall you come out on top.

Remember the Twitter account hijacking story we examined at the start of this chapter? The hackers used their access to high-profile Twitter accounts to convince people to transfer bitcoin to them. Now, the accounts they hijacked had millions upon millions of followers among them, meaning the fraudulent tweets would have been spread far and wide. Of course, the majority of people who saw those tweets recognized that they were probably the result of a hack, or at least were suspicious enough not to instantly go and transfer the bitcoin in the short time before Twitter secured those accounts and deleted the tweets. But it was never the hackers' intention to fool *everyone*; rather, they needed to fool just enough people to make the hack worthwhile. When all was said and done, enough people had bought into the tweets and transferred bitcoin to leave the hackers in possession of hundreds of thousands of dollars. That is the power of large-scale social engineering.

SIMPLE MISTAKES

Some years ago I worked with Peter Kim (a fellow hacker) to take advantage of one of the most common and overlooked human elements of data systems—typos—and then report on the consequences of doing so. We figured that it would be pretty common for people sending emails to each other to sometimes misspell the email address. Most particularly, if they were to misspell the domain part of the email, the email would be sent to the wrong location. To take a completely random example, it's not inconceivable that someone sending an internal email within the company of fakecompany.com might, if they were in a hurry and not being super attentive, mistype the end of the email as fakecompany.co or fakecompny.com or any number of misspellings. Now, if I were to go and register those domains in anticipation of such mistakes, I'd be able to receive any emails sent there. The sender wouldn't even be aware unless they went back and noticed the typo in the email they'd sent. Taking this approach and registering a whole number of "doppelganger domains," we managed to receive thousands of emails from a range of Fortune 500 companies, before publishing our findings in a report.

This technique has been used in some interesting ways. For example, in the mid-2000s a man named Christopher Lamparello registered the domain www.fallwell.com, anticipating that some people would misspell the surname of evangelical preacher Jerry Falwell, and used the site to attract his followers and to criticize some of Falwell's views. A more recent and more humorous example comes from 2018, when Rudy Giuliani neglected to put a space between two sentences in a tweet, ending up with the phrase "G-20.In" being analyzed as a link. A web developer in Arizona was quick to capitalize on this,

registering the domain and using it for a website with some antagonistic messaging.

And we're all prone to making such simple mistakes. I had a friend
who had his credit card cloned, but he didn't realize it for months.
The thing is, he mainly used that card for Amazon purchases, and his
statement wouldn't give details about the products he'd bought; it
would just list "Amazon." The person who cloned his card also used it
mainly for Amazon purchases, so whenever my friend glanced at his
statements and saw a whole bunch of transactions from Amazon, he
just assumed they were his usual purchases. It wasn't until the end
of the year when he saw his balance was about $20,000 more than it
should have been that the penny dropped. Had he been a little more
thorough when looking over his credit card statements, he might
have realized sooner and stopped the thief from stealing thousands
of dollars' worth of goods.

Whether we like it or not, and whether people recognize it or not,
the tendency to make simple mistakes is a common human trait and
as such is something that can easily be taken advantage of, particularly because people consistently underestimate their propensity
for making such mistakes and tend to minimize them when they do.
It's a human failing, stemming from a mixture of pride, embarrassment, and trust in oneself, and as such it's something that can be
taken advantage of by applying the hacker mindset. When Peter and
I worked on that report, you wouldn't be able to imagine the number of sensitive emails we received from some of the most prominent
companies in the country. Even after we published the report, the
reaction we encountered was largely one of frank disbelief. People
just couldn't accept that anyone would be so careless with confidential information—this is the human tendency to overlook small mistakes at play. But the fact is they do, and when they do you can use
that to your advantage.

INFILTRATION

A final point when it comes to this principle is that of infiltration—that is to say, you often need to become part of a system in order to influence it.

There are many ways in which you can make yourself part of a system. One common technique used by hackers is that of "sock puppets." These are fake accounts on social media platforms that can be used to infiltrate particular groups or communities. It's very easy to make a profile on LinkedIn listing a fake name, fake employment, and education history. Then all you have to do is go around liking posts of the people whose social circles you want to infiltrate. You can use the search to target employees of a particular company or people with a particular job title. As they start to see your false name pop up every time you like one of their posts you start to enter into their mind, and they start to feel favorably toward you. Eventually you connect with them, you start to message, and they trust you more and more. Then finally you're in the perfect position to gain whatever information you want from the person. Sound familiar? Well, it's pretty much the same technique as catfishing, only you're not tricking someone to fall in love with you.

This is just one way in which hackers use infiltration to gain access to what they want. Infiltration also works in person, of course. Remember earlier in this chapter where I talked about gaining access to a building by dressing up as a laborer? That's also a form of infiltration, because you're making the security guard think that you're one of their "group," that group being the people who are allowed legitimate access to the building. Another thing that people do is dress up as garbage removers to gain access to garbage where there may be (and to be honest very often is) sensitive information to be found.

Being seen as a part of the group is always going to help you get what you want from that group. To take this idea to a completely different place, let's say you're the new manager in an office and you've got all these great ideas to change the way things work. If you just charge in there and start telling everyone that they need to start doing things a certain way, you're going to get nowhere fast. People will naturally resist what they would see as an outsider who has come to impose new practices on them. But if you take a little time to connect with the people in the team and make them see you as one of them, they will be much more likely to go along with any changes you want to implement.

A lot of us have these social infiltration skills already. When we attend house parties or dinner parties, and generally when we meet new people, we automatically try to attune ourselves to the new group and make ourselves fit in. In fact, I think some of the people who are best at this are those people who grew up as the children of military parents. Usually those kids would move from one school to the next year after year, and so they'd be forced to learn how to fit in with new groups of people as quickly as possible. If you have such a background, you might have something of a head start on this, but the fact remains that the social skills required for infiltration are something that we all have.

I'm not a child of military parents, but I have been infiltrating social groups since my childhood. When I was at high school there was this group of super cool skater dudes who would spend all of their time tumbling about half-pipes at the skate park or smoking behind the sheds on the school campus. I really wanted to hang out with them, but I wasn't a smoker and couldn't skate to save my life. So what did I do? Well, I just started hanging out in the smoking area behind the sheds. I didn't smoke myself, but just being there meant I was hanging in the same place as, and by default with, the cool skate dudes. I didn't need to be doing the same things, but being in the same place gave me a chance to infiltrate the group, and I soon counted many of them among my friends.

But whether it's through infiltration, large-scale social engineering, or straightforward engagement with people, what lies at the core of all of these techniques is that people always have blind spots, preconceptions, and assumptions. By applying the hacker mindset in the context of social engineering, you can take advantage of those gaps and make them work for you.

Chapter 9

HACKER PRINCIPLE 6: PIVOT

The last hacker principle I want to discuss is about reacting to changing environments and making the most out of unexpected circumstances. Good plans only ever last for as long as it takes for the first problem to arise. The question is, what do you do then? There are many people who will grow disheartened and give up in the face of unexpected adversity; however, a key feature of hackers is that they will not only pivot to overcome such problems but will often take advantage of the unexpected situation to further achieve their goals. Remember the pendulum that represents the hacker mindset, swinging back and forth between planning and execution. The hacker principle of pivoting is a great instance of that pendulum in action.

A key aspect to making use of the unexpected lies in recognizing how all the various parts of a process have value. It can be very easy to view an endeavor as being composed purely of a method and a goal, the method being nothing more than a means to the end. The reality is, however, that very often there will be many aspects of the process that will provide you further advantages or tools to achieve your goal, or that will help you in achieving an alternative goal. Recognizing how those various advantages attained during the journey can be leveraged is often what sets hackers apart from those who do not adopt the hacker mindset.

A classic example of this would be a hacker trying to hack into a large retail company. Trying to hack straight in and get access to sensitive corporate information can be difficult, as more defense focus is there. After many attempts of trying to break into the internal systems, all they've managed to do is to hack their way into one of the store's cash registers. That's a failure, right? Wrong! Although getting into the cash register wasn't the hacker's goal, it is on the same network as the rest of the system and so could be used as a jumping point from which the hacker attempts additional attacks from that slightly more trusted cash register machine. As such, the successful hacker would see this not as a failure but as another step toward achieving success. This is what hackers call pivoting—recognizing the value of what you've attained so far and using it to change the direction of travel to achieve your goal.

PLUS, MINUS, MULTIPLY

No, it's not a compilation of Ed Sheeran's greatest hits—plus, minus, multiply represents the various ways in which you might pivot, building on and modulating what you've already achieved. Often, this comes down to looking at your previous or current approach to a particular project, seeing what works and what doesn't, and determining how the process needs to be adjusted to be more effective. It's a bit like cooking a dish. Perhaps you're cooking a stew and you have a taste as it's simmering away. It tastes a bit flat so you determine that you need to add some more salt or spices. Or perhaps it tastes *too* salty—well, in that case it might be a bit difficult to take salt out of the stew, but you'll know next time you're cooking it to add less salt. Or maybe you've left it to simmer for a few hours and it turns out that you've ended up with a lot less stew than you'd expected given the amount of ingredients you used. Next time, you'll know to use more ingredients. In each case you're learning from the experience and adjusting your approach accordingly. Very often, pivoting is simply a case of identifying what needs to be added to the mix (plus), what needs to be taken away (minus), or what needs to be amplified (multiply).

Coming back to the world of computer hacking, let's look at a quick example from my days working as a cybersecurity operative. My team and I were testing the security of the IT setup of a company whose entire system was cloud based, which meant it was all basically on the internet. They had a firewall in place to keep out unauthorized web traffic and as such they considered it to be an internal system, but essentially it was a public system with some restrictions in place. Our job was to see how the system would stand up against cyberattacks. Our extensive testing of the system from within the company meant we actually had a good understanding of how the system worked and where many of its vulnerabilities were. We had a robust plan of attack that would bring the system down, with only one problem: it would work only from within the company. Any external operator would be stopped from putting the attack plan into action by the firewall. So what we had was a good strategy, but it was missing a way in which to overcome the firewall. All we had to do was add that element to the plan and it would work. We eventually realized that we could add in a web header to the attack that would trick the firewall into believing that the web traffic was coming from a trusted IP, thus giving us access and, voilà, we were able to perform the attack and gain access to an internal system with sensitive information from the general internet. All our effort needed to be successful was for us to step back and think about how an essentially unworkable plan could be altered.

And thinking about things in this way can be applied to all kinds of contexts. Let's say you're running online ads for your business and because it's all online you've got good data on how well the various ad streams are working. You see that the ad banners you've been putting up on various websites are actually not driving very much traffic to your online store, though the email ads you've been sending out have been really quite successful. In that scenario, it would be a case of pivoting by removing the website banner ads from your overall marketing strategy and focusing on email ads. For another example, imagine you're crowdfunding for a new venture. You've done everything you can think of, you've built up hype on social media, reached out to and collaborated with various influencers, campaigned using email lists, and you've raised a fair amount of money, but you're still $10,000 short of your target. Here it would be a case of looking at what you've done and working out what's missing—that is to say, what could you add to the mix to make up the difference? Maybe it's simply a question of looking for an investor who'd be willing to help you achieve your target. And a third example might be that you're doing very well with your small business and bringing in a healthy profit, but you're limited by the scale at which you're operating. Here pivoting would take the form of amplifying what you're doing to take your business to the next level. This is the "multiply" side of pivoting, when you just need to turn up what you're doing to eleven. In fact, this can also be part of a great strategy when you're not sure exactly what to do; you could try a variety of things in a small way, doing little tests, as it were, and when you find which one works you just multiply on that.

What lies at the heart of all this is the ability to step back, look at what you're currently doing, and see how things can be improved by asking yourself these three simple questions: What could be added? What could be taken away? What could be amplified?

It's important to remember to keep a broad perspective on things when considering how to pivot. It's often the case that a pivot might involve a different area than where you've been focusing. When we talked about reverse engineering, we considered looking at things through the lenses of people, process, and technology. When reviewing your current endeavors, it might be the case, for example, that you've got the technology right, but you need to make an addition on the process side. Pivoting doesn't mean you have to stick within the parameters in which you've already been operating, but it does mean varying your approach based on what you've already accomplished. So much of the process of applying this hacker principle comes from simply adding, removing, multiplying, mixing things up, and trying again. Just because things haven't gone quite according to plan doesn't mean you're failing—often it's simple permutations of what you're already doing that will lead you to success.

CONNECTING THE DOTS

So far I've talked about pivoting in relation to instances where things are not going according to plan and you're not achieving your goals. However, hackers will often incorporate the idea of pivoting into their plans from the outset. This is because there are usually many, many attack paths that will lead hackers to their goals, and hackers know that even if they don't have a clear path to their end goal to start with, once they're in the thick of working toward their goal, opportunities of which they can take advantage will arise. I like to think of it as a process of connecting dots—the hacker starts at the beginning, at the end lies the system they're trying to hack, and in between them is a myriad of attack points and opportunities. The only question is how many of those points the hacker will connect until they work out their successful attack path that will get them to their ultimate goal.

Remember how I talked about hacking into a store's cash register, and how this could help a hacker get into the internal corporate network of the retail store? Well, that's actually quite a good strategy to take from the outset, because the cash register is going to have weaker security than the crucial systems in the network. Hospitals are unfortunately notoriously vulnerable in this sense, because they often have digital signs or readout systems for patients in the waiting queue that have lower security but are still part of the broader network of the hospital. Hackers know that if they hack those low-security points they will probably yield greater opportunities to hack the whole system.

Another variation of this is known as "water-hole attacks." This is where a hacker wants to hack a particular system composed of end users, and so the hacker will hack various websites the users visit and use them to infect those users' computers, bringing them closer to their goals. All strategies involve going after the more vulnerable points associated with a system and having the confidence that they will yield results that will allow you to move closer to your end goal, as well as the ability to take advantage of those results and pivot accordingly.

You'd be surprised at how far moving from one dot to the next can take you. Imagine if you were driving your car on a sunny Saturday afternoon and all of a sudden it began to do things all on its own. First the radio would change of its own accord, then the A/C kicks into high, and then the dashboard warns the car's transmission controls are off. It sounds like a scene from a nightmare, doesn't it? Well, the reality is it has actually happened. Not to an unsuspecting victim, you'll be happy to hear, but in a test to see just how far ethical hackers could go by connecting dots.

Charlie Miller and Chris Valasek were the hackers in question. It all started when they focused on the entertainment and navigation system of the Jeep Cherokee, noticing that it was connected to the internet and that anyone who knew the relevant IP address and ports could connect to the system remotely. Well, that's a bit bad, but not horrible—what's the worst that could happen? A sick-minded hacker breaking into the radio and making it play country music on repeat? There are worse things in the world. That might seem like a logical point of view, but you'd be dead wrong in taking it. The fact is that Miller and Valasek were able to go from the entertainment system to all the other parts of the car, including being able to turn off the transmission, disable the brakes, and even take control of the steering (though, for some reason, only when the car was in reverse). What they realized was something that won't be obvious to most people—the car was just a system of various parts connected to each other, and as we've seen through this book, taking advantage of systems is what hacking is all about. By pivoting from one part of the system to the next, they were eventually able to take control of pretty much the entire car while it was cruising along the highway—a terrifying thought!

Another example of how this kind of approach can work is the case of Anna Sorokin. You might remember her—she made the news some years ago for being at the center of a fraud scandal where she convinced a number of banks, hotels, and socialites in New York that she was a German heiress called Anna Delvey. It was a really intriguing story, so much so that they made a show on Netflix about her not too long ago. What really grabbed my attention when I heard about her story was the way in which she pivoted from one scenario to the next. Posing as this incredibly wealthy heiress, she mingled with various members of the glitterati in New York, and then used those connections and relationships to further back her story and to pursue a lavish lifestyle, despite having very little actual money to spend. Of course it would all eventually come crashing down around her (she's now in prison), and though I'd obviously not condone her extensive fraud, her story is a good example of how the hacker principles of pivoting and social engineering can work in a societal setting.

In all these cases what is key is making sure you're taking advantage of everything that presents itself to you in your journey. You may not have a clearly defined path to your goal to start with, and that's fine as long as you remain open to all the opportunities and possibilities that arise as you go along and seize them when they do.

It's worth bearing in mind here that though going along a path of connecting dots can be a very powerful way to reach your goal, it is also important to be mindful of whether or not it's worth the effort. In the previous chapter we looked at large-scale social engineering strategies, such as phishing, smishing, and pretexting. These are all techniques in which you cast your net out wide and get whatever access you end up getting. It's almost always then necessary to work from what you get to what you want through a series of pivots. That's all well and good, but there is also a technique that is the reverse of these large-scale social engineering attacks, and that's called spear phishing. Spear phishing involves specifically targeting users with the exact access you want, as opposed to the broad and untargeted attacks of large-scale social engineering campaigns. Both approaches have their merits, and the decision as to which to use comes down to a judgment as to which will be the most efficient. It might be that getting to your end goal would require so many pivots as to make it not worth it—in that case, spear phishing would be the better choice. It would involve more effort up front, but a smaller amount of effort in pivots would make it worth it. The important point to emphasize here is that you must always remain realistic in your approach. Connecting dots and getting to your goal through a series of pivots is certainly a great technique, but you must always remain conscious of whether it's the right technique for the scenario at hand.

AS THE OPPORTUNITIES ARISE

Let's stick with large-scale social engineering attacks for the time being. The purpose of such attacks is to gain access to a system, but the nature of a large-scale strategy like this is that you can't be sure exactly what kind of access you'll get. The key to making this work, then, is for the hacker to take advantage of any opportunities that they find once they've gained some kind of access. Since they can't be sure precisely what this will be, they'll need to be agile in making use of whatever becomes available to them. This is at the heart of hacker-level pivoting and, of course, as with computer hacking so with everything else.

Successful entrepreneurs and business owners often pivot to take advantage of the opportunities that come about as part of the process of pursuing their goals. Take a salesperson, for example. A big part of selling involves putting the potential buyer in the frame of mind where they're willing to part with their money. As a salesperson, you'd probably be doing this by enthusing about the benefits of purchasing whatever product you're selling, but what separates a decent sales-person from a great salesperson is that the great salesperson will then pivot. They've just put all this effort into getting the purchaser to spend their money—why not take advantage of that? The customer is now in "buying mode," so it's time to sell more, going beyond what they had originally intended to buy. "Oh, well now that you're buying this TV, you might want this stand and soundbar to go with it," or "I can see you're really excited to buy this TV, but why not just spend a few more hundred dollars and get this even better version?" The key to cross-selling and upselling lies in taking advantage of all the groundwork you've done in getting the customer to the point of pur-chasing and pushing it as far as it will go.

Another great example of someone who has seized opportuni-ties as they arose and pivoted his career again and again is famous YouTuber and doctor Ali Abdaal. He started off as a medical doctor, and then decided to use all his experience studying for and passing the various medical exams to guide others in their attempts to pass those exams, taking to YouTube to do so and eventually founding the company 6med with this precise aim. He'd eventually leave medical practice to focus on his career as an influencer and entrepreneur. But what's particularly interesting is, having worked on his YouTube career, he then began to use *this* experience to teach others about how to make a career in social media. He's been a great pivoter—it seems like every time he develops a skill set for a particular goal, he decides to make a career out of sharing that skill set with others rather than focusing on the goal he originally had in mind. And it's clearly worked very well for him, which underlines another important lesson underpinning the principle of pivoting: the goal that serves you best is not necessarily the goal you set out for at the start. Being aware of where the various opportunities can take you and being ready to follow them is another important part of applying this hacker principle in your life.

This approach can also pay major dividends when thinking about career development. If there's a certain job at a particular company you want, it might be pretty difficult to just go for that job off the bat. However, if you manage to get a different job in the company, you'll find that it will be a lot easier to move around within the system once you're inside. Getting your foot in the door, then seeing what opportunities you find as you move toward your preferred position, could be a much more viable strategy than simply going straight for the role at the beginning.

This reminds me of the career entrepreneur and venture capitalist Chris Sacca. Fairly early on in his career he was working for Google as corporate counsel, and he would frequently volunteer to record the minutes for various high-level meetings. Being in those meetings would give him access to various high-level individuals, connections he would be able to leverage to further his career. Of course, it would also eventually change his perspective on what he wanted to do and propel him into the world of capital investment, where he invested in a number of tech companies, again building on and leveraging that experience he developed while working at Google.

My own career is another great example of pivoting in action. As an employee working as an ethical hacker, I built up a huge amount of insight into what hackers want and crucially where the pain points in their day-to-day activities are. When I started my business, I was able to leverage all that knowledge in order to offer consumers working in the cybersecurity industry exactly the things they wanted, which was the key to my success.

And this is what the hacker principle of pivoting is all about—being aware of all the experience, information, and opportunities you attain as you proceed toward your goals. Furthermore, it involves making sure you take full advantage of them, whether in achieving your original aims or changing direction and looking toward even higher plateaus.

Part III

THE HACKER
MINDSET APPLIED

Chapter 10

THE HACKER METHODOLOGY

Having established the hacker principles, as well as the characteristics of a hacker, we're now going to bring them together and see how they can be put to use in a systematic and productive way. This is what the hacker methodology is—a process whereby you utilize the hacker characteristics and principles to help you achieve your goals. In terms of a structure, it's a little like the scientific method, which involves forming a hypothesis and then moving from one step to another in order to prove it, with subsequent iterations used to validate and improve the theory. The hacker methodology is similar, except instead of forming a hypothesis we'll be identifying objectives and then moving from there to achieve those objectives. The methodology is also cyclical and iterative, which gives it particular strength because it means you're always improving your journey, both in terms of achieving your goals and optimizing the path toward them. The important point to underline here is that it's a method—that is to say, it's a systematic process where we go from one step to the next to ensure that the goals are achieved.

Without further ado, then, let's delve straight into the five steps of the hacker methodology.

1: OBJECTIVE

Knowing what you want is always the first step toward achieving it, and that's why determining your objective is the first step in the hacker methodology. Naturally, you have to know what your goal is before you can go about pursuing it, and as I've mentioned in previous chapters, knowing what you want isn't always as trivial as some may think. Working out the precise parameters of your goals can often be half the battle, and spending a lot of time working through the methodology only to realize that the objective isn't really what you want can result in quite a lot of wasted effort, so it's worth taking the time to ensure you get it right from the outset. Working toward an objective with a clear goal in mind is always going to pay greater dividends than simply trying to work it out as you go along.

The hacker principles to bear in mind for this step are those of being on offense and risk. The former comes into play as you consider the possibilities of what you can achieve. Too many people suffer from timidity when they set goals for themselves. More often than not, the limits of your ability are far beyond what you might initially assume. For example, if you've decided that your goal is to earn a six-figure salary, that's what you'll be focusing on, and your mind will remain in that area. Obviously earning a seven-figure salary would always be better than earning six figures. The difference between $100k a year and $1 million a year is huge, and it might well be the case that you're more than capable of getting to that one million mark, but if you've set your objective lower it's likely that you won't even be thinking about it. Your brain will be calibrated to the goal you've set, and you'll think differently if you have bigger goals in mind than if you have smaller goals. Don't limit yourself with modest objectives. When setting your objectives, being on offense will open up the parameters of what's achievable and allow you to set your visions as high as possible.

At the same time, it's necessary to be realistic about your goals (remember the hacker characteristic of being realistic), and this is where thinking about risk comes in. Having asked yourself what you can achieve with no boundaries in mind, you need to move on to ask yourself which goals are actually worth pursuing, which will be the most rewarding, and which will require too much effort for too little return. Bearing in mind the balance between effort and return, which is a key part of assessing risk, will help you ensure that your objectives will be the most worthwhile for you personally.

Warren Buffett is known for having this thing called the 5/25 rule. The story goes that an airline pilot once asked him how to get everything in his life done. Buffett responded by telling him to write down twenty-five professional goals and then to circle the five most important of them. He'd then have two lists, the list of five top-priority goals and the list of twenty less important goals. Crucially, he'd then disregard the list of less important goals and focus solely on those top five priorities. What makes the 5/25 rule so effective is that it makes you acknowledge that you can't do everything, allowing yourself to focus on your top priorities while consciously *not* pursuing the less important goals, meaning you have the bandwidth to actually achieve the goals you most want to. Thinking about this more broadly, you also want to make sure that you're not overburdened. Though the idea of working oneself to the limits of one's capacity might be appealing to some people, it's not actually a good strategy. Unexpected things are always going to crop up in your life, and you need to make sure that you have the space to deal with them without compromising your objectives. The only way to be sure of this is to make sure that your objectives are not consuming all your time and that, should it become necessary, you can dedicate some time to other matters.

It would be good to spend a couple of moments here thinking about the scope of your objectives. A key feature of hackers is that they often take a step back and observe the long-term view. Black-hat hackers who are trying to break into a computer system are often happy to sit on the network for years, biding their time as they wait for the opportune moment to strike. Ethical hackers who are trying to stop this from happening therefore need to have a similarly long-term view in order to remain on top. Keeping one's mind on the long term is an important part of achieving robust and enduring success—after all, there's no point in briefly achieving a particular goal before finding yourself in exactly the same position you were in before. Unfortunately, we are in an age of short-term thinking, a philosophy constantly pushed down our throats by a society that values instant gratification above all else and that sees people constantly looking for the next dopamine hit without much thought for the longer-term implications. To achieve enduring success, it is necessary to rise above this and think about the long term in setting your objectives.

Finally, I want you to bear in mind that the hacker methodology is recursive. We'll see this a little later in this chapter, but this is relevant when it comes to setting objectives because it means you can incorporate sub-objectives, which can come together into a macro-objective. It may be that what you ultimately want to achieve requires pursuing other goals in the shorter term—the methodology allows for this, so don't be afraid of setting mini-objectives that will in the end lead you to your main objective.

So, bearing all of that in mind, what are the objectives that you want to set out to achieve? Once you know that, you can begin the reconnaissance stage.

2: RECONNAISSANCE

Amat victoria curam. Victory loves preparation. That's an ancient proverb that finds its origins in the peak of the Roman Republic, just before Julius Caesar would begin to transform the republic into an empire. It's also a proverb that embodies the second step of the hacker methodology: reconnaissance.

With the objective established, it's time to start gathering the information that will allow you to achieve that objective. In the reconnaissance stage of the hacker methodology you start to figure out what you need in order to attain your goals. Naturally, this will draw heavily on the principle of reverse engineering, because analyzing the systems at play will reward you with a wealth of information with regard to how those systems work and how they can be manipulated. As we discussed in the reverse engineering chapter, you should look at the problems at hand through the lenses of PPT, identifying the various people, processes, and technology involved, and considering how they can bring you closer to your objective.

The other principle to bring into play here is living off the land. Remember how we spoke about hackers making use of freely available resources from the ecosystem such as open-source software projects? That's just the tip of the iceberg when it comes to thinking about the amount of information and resources that is available. The fact is, there are so many people, both online and offline, who are aggregating knowledge, and it follows that a big part of the reconnaissance stage is to get hold of that information. Throughout this stage you will need to remain mindful of how easy it is to attain the information you need and be proactive in accumulating it. Bearing your objectives in mind, you just need to go out and start asking questions. Are there people or companies who have achieved similar objectives that you can model yourself on? If so, what did they do, and what resources did they make use of? Are you a consumer of a product relating to your objectives? If so, what insights can you bring from your experiences to bear on your objectives? In chapter five, we looked at Michael Dell and how he reverse-engineered an Apple computer, ultimately founding Dell Computers. He started off as just another consumer of computers, but he would then go on to use his familiarity with the product to become a successful entrepreneur.

Just to give an example of how easy it can be to attain the information you need, let's have a quick look back at the story of how I discovered a zero-day hack of a sophisticated funds-transfer system. A zero-day hack is a software vulnerability that, at the point of being discovered, is unknown by the company, developers, admins, or users of the software. As you can imagine, such vulnerabilities are particularly valuable to computer hackers, since they can be used to develop attacks that no one sees coming, so discovering one is a pretty big deal. I talked about this story in the risk chapter, but to briefly recap: there was this electronic funds-transfer system that was largely considered to be secure, and I decided to find out exactly how secure it was. So I went off and I did my reconnaissance, and a big part of that simply involved reading the program's manual, which was of course freely available. I read the whole thing from cover to cover and used it to look at the system from multiple perspectives, such as that of the developer and that of the end user. Simply by reading that manual and interrogating it thoroughly, I was able to discover attack points that nobody thought of, which ultimately allowed me to break into the system.

And as we saw when we looked at the principle of living off the land, resources are plentiful, and nowhere more so than on the internet. There are plenty of specialized communities on the internet, such as on Reddit and Stack Overflow, that can answer any questions you have, and probably have done so already. As long as you're asking the right questions, the answers are usually relatively easy to find—more often than not, they're just a couple of Google searches away. Some of the more complex questions may not be answered so simply, however, but then as AI technology develops, more sophisticated resources become available.

In November 2022, OpenAI released ChatGPT, which is a chat engine that uses machine learning and artificial intelligence to answer questions. Its ability to problem-solve is really astounding. I have a friend who was working on some code recently, and he asked ChatGPT to solve an issue he was having with it, which it promptly did. Then he told it that the code had another problem, and then another, and another, and each time ChatGPT would look for problems, identify them, and suggest solutions. Before he knew it, the Chat was finding and solving problems that he hadn't even realized were there.

Another important point to bring back here is the idea of the pendulum we spoke about in chapter two. It can be very easy to get caught up in reconnaissance and lose sight of the broader picture. Remember, the purpose of the methodology is not simply to understand the system as fully as possible, but to achieve your aims. Reconnaissance is an important part of that process, but it's only one part and a true hacker is always aware of the need to balance planning with execution. As such, the amount of reconnaissance you must undertake needn't be comprehensive, it just has to be enough to meet your needs—and the next stage of the hacker methodology is where you make that determination.

3: ANALYSIS

At step three of the hacker methodology we're still essentially in the planning stage, but now we're working out precisely how our goals can be achieved. Now that we've gathered all that information in the reconnaissance stage, it's time to really interrogate that data to work out how it can be used to get to your objective. Of course, you'll be bearing in mind all the hacker principles as you work out the best ways in which your knowledge of the systems involved can be used to reach your goal, but one of them I would like to highlight here is that of risk. At the objective stage we used this principle to work out realistic and worthwhile goals. Now, having done the reconnaissance and being armed with greater knowledge, you may find that the parameters for what you calculate to be worthwhile have changed.

At this stage it's very good to remember the principle of pivoting. Remember how we talked about pivoting as the process of connecting the dots that hackers go through as they work out the best and most efficient attack paths? That's exactly what you'll be doing at this stage of the hacker methodology. What exactly is the process you'll need to go through in order to get to your goal? What are the vulnerabilities in the systems you've studied as part of the reconnaissance stage that you'll be able to take advantage of? In what order should you make use of these exploits? Working out your own attack path is an important part of the analysis step of the methodology.

Let's look at an example. You're a computer hacker trying to break into a computer system, and as part of your reconnaissance you've learned that the system has two servers—a production server, which is the main server used by the system, and a test server, which the organization developers use to make sure anything new they want to implement will work fine. Both servers have the data you want to gain access to. The analysis comes in recognizing that since the production server is the one that's in use, it's going to have much higher security than the test server. They wouldn't be expecting the test server to be the subject of an external attack. As such, you work out that going after the test server is your best course of action. In short, analysis is taking the information you've learned and transforming it into an actual plan.

Transforming the raw data acquired during reconnaissance into a workable plan of action can of course be quite difficult. After all, that information often isn't presented in a neatly categorized format but rather comes as a mass of disparate facts. Using diagrams and tables to visualize that data can be super helpful at this point. You might want to make use of something like the four-quadrant Eisenhower Matrix—a diagram that is often used to help people with time management and prioritization. The matrix categorizes all the tasks in relation to two criteria: urgent or non-urgent tasks and important or unimportant tasks. Everything can be categorized as something that needs to be done first (urgent and important), something that needs to be scheduled (non-urgent and important), something that can be delegated (urgent and unimportant), or something that can be ignored (non-urgent and unimportant).

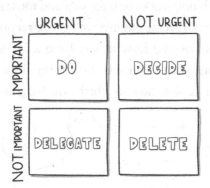

Of course, I'm not saying that this precise type of analysis is going to be useful in every situation, but the four-quadrant approach is actually quite versatile and very useful in helping one to organize the data in a more easily analyzable format.

For example, entrepreneur Ramit Sethi used the same principles to create the product demand matrix, rating businesses based on their audiences and the dollar value of their products. The important thing is to visualize the data in such a way that it becomes clearly comprehensible, allowing you to more easily work out your attack path to achieving your objective.

HIGH PRICE

HIGH END	GOLDEN GOOSE
LABOR of LOVE	MASS MARKET

FEW CUSTOMERS

MANY CUSTOMERS

LOW PRICE

With all this information sorted out, you'll be well placed to work out your attack path, or your path of action. There are often various possible paths that will lead to success, but the analysis step is where you work out which one works best for you and most suits your needs. Using the principle of reverse engineering at the reconnaissance stage, you might have discovered how others have achieved the objective you've set. That's one path to success. Now is the time to look at all the other possible paths and decide on which you are going to take.

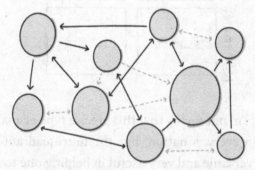

4: EXECUTION

This is the stage that all the strategy and planning has been working up to. You've decided on your objective, you've gathered all the relevant information, and you've analyzed that information to work out your plan of action. Now it's time to execute that plan. Once again, let's remember the pendulum of the hacker—we can't spend all our time planning; we need to balance that with execution, and this is the stage of the hacker methodology where that comes into effect. It can be daunting, but there comes a point where you just need to say, *Let's do this, and go ahead with it.* Writers encounter this turning point very often; as a writer it can be very tempting to spend all your time planning out what's going to be in your book. Many writers kind of feel like a big part of their job involves walking round and round the garden thinking. However, as any successful writer will tell you, the only real job of a writer is to glue one's ass to the chair and write.

Having the confidence to move on from the planning stage and just get on with the execution isn't always easy. You need to have faith in your abilities and in the process. You've done the reconnaissance; you've done the analysis—trusting in the process will give you the freedom to put your plan into action without being plagued by doubt. It's important to avoid second-guessing your plan. It's natural for humans to feel doubts when beginning something new, but constantly wondering whether your plan is correct is keeping the pendulum too far on the planning side. The best plan in the world is no good at all if it's not executed. This reminds me of a quote from Napoleon Hill: "Action is the real measure of intelligence." It doesn't matter how clever you've been in gathering all the relevant information and analyzing it. If you don't actually put it to use, it's just the same as not having done anything at all.

It's also important to think about the speed of execution. In computer hacking it's generally quite easy to do things speedily, because you can often do quite a lot of things in a short time. However, even if you can do things quickly, you still can't do everything, so you have to prioritize and make sure you're focusing on the most important elements of your project. More generally in life, you need to be realistic in regard to what can be achieved in a given time. However, you don't want to miss out on opportunities to achieve your objective because you've allowed the best moment to slip by. Striking while the iron is hot can be a key part of making sure your objective is achieved.

5: REASSESS

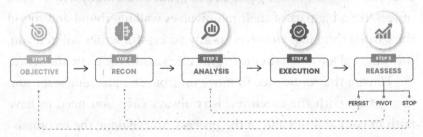

This is the final step in the hacker methodology, and it's a step that gives the whole process much more potency. Okay, you've gone through each of the stages—you've decided on your objective, you've gathered all the relevant information, you've analyzed that information and come up with a plan, and you've put that plan into action. Now what? Well, you might think that you've either achieved your objective or you haven't. The reality is that it's usually not so straightforward.

If you've achieved your objective, well, that's great, but life doesn't end there. It's time to ask yourself: What next? Where do you go from here? Things will have changed, so you'll need to step back and take stock of where the facts stand at the moment. Now that you've reached this point, what's your next objective going to be? Or it may be that you've achieved your original objective to some degree, but not completely. Is it worthwhile to keep on going on the same path? At which point do you reach the point of diminishing returns? Remember when I mentioned the Pareto principle back when I was talking about the characteristic of being efficient—the principle that 80 percent of outcomes come from 20 percent of causes? If that 80 percent of outcomes is achieved, is it worth putting in the rest of the other 80 percent of effort for that extra 20 percent of results? It may very well not be; sometimes, the smartest move is to quit while you're ahead.

And, of course, there's always the possibility that you've gone through the process and not achieved your objective. In that case, now's the time to step back and work out why not. Remember what we talked about when we looked at the principle of pivoting? When things don't go the way you expect, it's often the case that only some small adjustments are needed to make it work. You may need to identify what's missing from the plan that can be added in, or what's superfluous that can be taken away, or whether some element needs to be amplified. This stage of the hacker methodology gives you the opportunity to zoom out and work out precisely what alterations to the strategy are needed to achieve success. And once again, remember the pendulum—yes, one side of the pendulum is making sure you don't spend all your time planning and never putting that plan into action, but the other is not getting completely caught up in execution while neglecting developments in the plan. The key to the pendulum is finding the balance between both planning and execution mode, and swinging back and forth from one to the other.

Finally, I just want to make a note again of the recursive nature of this methodology—the final step brings you back to the first. Hackers are always in a sort of arms race with each other, black-hat hackers looking for exploits and vulnerabilities and ethical hackers working to head off those exploits and vulnerabilities. The recursive nature of the hacker methodology is key to how hackers ensure that they always remain ahead of the game. Things invariably change, so constantly cycling through this process is the way to keep on top. As I mentioned, life doesn't come to an end just because you've achieved an objective—things will keep on happening and you'll want to continue to develop and succeed as they do. Reassessing the situation, seeing what's changed, and using that to formulate your new goals is the way to ensure continued and enduring success.

Now that we've gone through each step of the hacker methodology, let's have a look at how it can be applied in some common scenarios. First off, we'll look at how the hacker methodology can be used to advance your career.

Chapter 11

CORPORATE CAREER

✖

HACKER MINDSET

I want to tell you a story about a kid I was at school with. His name was Paul.

Paul was full of hope and aspiration when he graduated college. He was the kind of person who had always been at the top of the pile. In high school he was one of the popular kids while managing to get top grades without putting in any effort. He thrived at college, passing his classes with no problem, and he certainly made the most of college life. Everything had always worked out for him and he had no reason to suspect things would be any different in his post-college life. He wasn't completely sure what kind of job he wanted to get, but he'd been a math major so he was sure that whatever it was he'd end up doing, it would be good. He'd always been told that STEM graduates ended up with the best careers, after all.

So he started applying for jobs, rather haphazardly at first, and for a few months he got no responses whatsoever. Eventually he began to get interviews and after a little while he landed a job in the middle office of an investment bank. *Sweet*, he thought. *It's all smooth sailing from here.* He was a diligent worker and after a couple of years he managed to get a promotion, along with a moderate pay increase. More years passed by and he continued to work hard, his labors being rewarded by regular, if modest, pay raises, but his career never really took off the way he'd imagined. At the end of each day he'd come home completely drained and veg out in front of the television—sometimes he'd fall asleep right there on the couch. Fifteen years later and Paul was still there, working away and wondering where he'd gone wrong.

There are Pauls all over the place. It's so easy for people to get stuck in careers they hate, or that are simply mediocre and that fail to excite them. As I talked about in the beginning of this book, I was one of those people. In this chapter we're going to look at some of the reasons people end up with unsatisfying and stagnant careers, and how the hacker mindset and methodology can be applied to avoid that scenario if you're just starting out in your career, or how to escape from it if you've found yourself stuck.

THE PROS AND CONS OF EMPLOYED WORK

The first question you need to ask yourself is if being an employee is the right choice for you. For me it wasn't, which is why my path to fulfillment meant leaving that world behind and focusing on being an independent entrepreneur. But that's not going to be the case for everyone, and for many people having a career as a salaried employee is the right choice. If that's the case for you, this chapter is about how to make that work.

In considering this question we can use the hacker characteristic of being realistic to think about the benefits and pitfalls of being an employee. There are quite a few negative aspects of employed work that have to be taken into account, at the top of which lies the insurmountable fact that companies and corporations don't care about their employees. Many of them will make a show of being caring and considerate, and of having values, but the fact is the only thing that matters to a corporation is the bottom line on the profit and loss sheet. If you're going to be an employee you'll have to be resolved to stand up and take care of your own interests, because the company itself isn't going to do that.

This even extends to the HR department of most companies. On the surface it may seem that HR at the very least should be the part of the company that cares about the employees, since they're the ones who are going to have the policies in place that are supposed to protect the employees' well-being. However, the reality is they're only there to maintain the corporate system whose sole objective is to maximize profits. You might find, then, that promotions and pay raises are hard to come by, even if you are rightly deserving of them. Many companies have policies of not promoting people too often, so for example if you got a promotion last year they may not consider you for one the following year by default, or they may limit the number of promotions available. It may be that if there are one hundred employees in a certain position there will only be five promotions available, so you'll be in direct (and often nasty) competition with your coworkers. This kind of system found its extreme in companies like Enron, which infamously had a policy whereby they would routinely fire the bottom 15 percent worst-performing employees. This kind of pseudo-Darwinian capitalist nightmare can't have been a healthy environment to exist in.

On the other hand, there are some notable benefits to being an employee of a company. Being an employee often means you have a level of stability and security that you won't find elsewhere.

Business owners and investors often have incomes that are reliant on the whims of the market—if things are going well, they can earn big, but it's also always possible that things go badly and they end up earning very little or even losing money. Being an employee means you don't take that risk and that at the end of every month you're guaranteed that paycheck. This kind of security can't be dismissed, and for some people it's the linchpin that means focusing on a career in employed work is the best option for them. This is particularly common when people have families and other commitments to take care of, where being able to rely on that regular income can be massively important.

Having a solid employment agreement can also provide stability in other ways. It will mean that the terms and parameters of your job (and therefore the way in which you earn money) are clearly set out and you won't be required to do things you're not expecting to do or wouldn't be happy doing. There can be a certain level of comfort and contentment involved in knowing precisely what you'll be having to do and being compensated for that with a reliable paycheck. In addition to that, being an employee often comes with benefits, whether that's paid time off, sick leave, or health insurance. These are all things you can't rely on if you're an independent business owner, for example.

And after all, there are some super successful people who chose to take the path of employed work. Some of these include Bob Iger, Tim Cook, Sheryl Sandberg, and Jony Ive. Yes, they're mainly chief executives, but they're all people who started off as regular employees and made their way to the top of their respective professions.

Taking all this into consideration, and thinking about the requirements of your particular circumstances and what personally is most important to you, you have to ask yourself if having a career as an employee is the right decision for you. If your answer to that question is yes, let's go on to look at how you can thrive in such a career.

WHAT DO YOU WANT
FROM YOUR CAREER?

As you'll remember from the previous chapter, the first step of the hacker methodology is determining your objectives. In this case it means asking what precisely it is that you want to optimize for when it comes to your career. What's most important to you? If it's mainly about the money, then you'll want to look at ways to maximize your income as an employee. If it's about having a prestigious job title and seniority, then you'll want to look at ways in which you can best progress up the ladder of promotions. Perhaps you're most concerned about your work-life balance, in which case you'll want to look at optimizing your strategy to give options in terms of flexible working. Maybe it's simply a question of job satisfaction and finding the work you do engaging, for which you'd be better off considering the best way to switch careers. Or it may be that you're concerned about the company's mission and you want to work for a purpose that you find yourself more aligned with. For all of these the hacker mindset can be used to develop and execute successful strategies that will improve your situation as an employee, but as usual it's important to ascertain from the outset precisely what it is you want to achieve as you go through the hacker methodology.

You'll also want to determine whether you want to optimize your position at your current job, or whether you'll want to transfer to a new one. Whether or not you choose to do so may depend on the other objectives that you've settled on, as you may find it will be necessary to take one or the other approach to satisfy those objectives. You may even be a recent graduate looking to get your first full-time job in the workplace. We'll be looking at tactics that will address all these possibilities. But all of this brings up another question when it comes to drawing objectives, which is: What are you willing to compromise on? For example, there may be a fantastic job that fulfills all the criteria of your objectives, but it requires you to relocate to another state. Are you willing to do that? There is of course no right or wrong answer to this—it all comes down to your own personal circumstances and preferences—but it does highlight the importance of knowing what you are and aren't willing to do. Establishing where your red lines are is almost as important as establishing what your objectives are, and only once you've determined this should you go on to the next step of the hacker methodology.

SALARIES AND PROMOTIONS

The first set of objectives I want us to look at are salaries and promotions. No matter how much corporations like to pressure their employees into acting like they're really motivated by the company and its goals, the fact is that 99 percent of people go to work because they want to be paid, and ultimately to be paid well. And there's nothing wrong with that! The question is, then, what can you do to maximize your earnings as an employee?

The first thing to say on this point is that promotions, bonuses, and salary increases aren't going to just fall into your lap. There's this pervasive idea that if you're loyal and hardworking you'll get all the rewards you deserve. However, this is absolutely not the case. Companies never want to pay a single cent more than they have to, and if they've got an employee who dutifully gets on with their work, consistently and quietly producing great results, why would they proactively spend more money on that person? The way they see it, they've already got that employee—after all, increasing their pay doesn't benefit the company. This means that if you want a pay raise or a bonus or promotion, you're going to have to go after it yourself. No one else is going to get those things for you—it's up to you.

The second point to note on this front is that in pursuing promotions and salary increases, you're inevitably going to be in competition with your colleagues. Usually companies have a set budget for bonuses and pay raises, and a limited number of promotions available—there might be one promotion available for every twenty employees, for example, and you can bet your bottom dollar that if you're after that promotion, so are many of your colleagues. If you're going to come out on top, you need to make sure that you stand out from the crowd.

Visibility is crucial in this case. You need to make sure that you're a person who is visible and known within the company. Being quietly competent is not good enough. Even if you're the number one top performer, if you're not being seen by others in the company, you're not going to be at the top of the list when bonuses and promotions are being considered. Of course, that doesn't mean you *shouldn't* be a strong performer—it's no good being well known in the company if you're well known for being a walking disaster—but you should be aware that your "brand" within the company can be as important as your individual output. Simply being vocal about your expertise and accomplishments (without being boastful, of course) can be a great way of increasing your visibility. For example, if you notice a colleague struggling with a particular problem that you know the solution to, get in there and help them, and then talk about it. Or, even better, if you come across a tricky problem in your own work and you know how to solve it, take the solution, rather than the problem, to your manager. There's a big difference between saying "I have this problem; what should I do?" and "There's this problem, and this is how I'm going to solve it." Being competent and being vocal about it is a sure way to ingrain your value into the minds of upper management, and when those opportunities for promotions or salary reviews or bonuses come up, your name is already going to be on the tips of their tongues.

Of course, another aspect of being visible and pursuing promotions and pay raises comes in simply asking for those things. Remember the hacker principles of being on offense and of determining risk—you need to go out there and chase those opportunities. Just asking for a pay raise is an instance of asymmetric risk, because the worst outcome is that they just say no, whereas the possibility of your being successful is substantial. And even if they say no, by asking for a pay raise or a promotion, you're making yourself more visible and making it clear to the leadership of the company that you're someone who wants to progress and move forward with your career. These are all things that will only benefit you in the long run.

The final point to note when it comes to optimizing for salary is to recognize how much loyalty does *not* correlate with an increase in pay. In fact, it correlates negatively, in that the more loyal you are to a company, the less likely it is that your pay will increase. The reason is obvious when you think about it—if you're a loyal employee, the company needs to spend less to keep you on board. This is actually a truism in all kinds of commercial and financial aspects of life, including energy companies, internet providers, and credit card companies. If you remain a loyal customer, you're going to have fewer benefits and probably pay more than those who switch companies. Not too long ago I was having quite a few problems with Amazon Prime—they kept getting my orders wrong, deliveries were delayed, and various orders arrived damaged. I phoned Amazon to complain and after a few minutes of venting the customer service person asked me if I wanted to cancel my Prime subscription. "No," I said, and the conversation petered out to no resolution. I realized at that point that they had me. If I wasn't willing to walk away, there was no incentive for them to invest any time or money to keep me on as a customer. I subsequently canceled my Prime membership and I've hardly noticed the difference.

Coming back to the question of careers, we can see from statistics that employees who fairly frequently move from one company to another do much better in terms of pay than those who don't. Changing companies can substantially increase your salary, with increases from around 20 to 40 percent, as opposed to a possible 5 to 10 percent pay increase you might expect to get by remaining in the same company. That's not to say you should be moving companies *too* often—employers tend to look askance at potential employees whose resumés are full of three-month stints at various organizations. The sweet spot is to look to move every two to three years. That's enough time to demonstrate that you're a serious employee while avoiding being stuck with stagnating pay in the same company for too long. After around ten years you'll see that your pay will easily outpace that of a peer who has remained loyal to a particular organization. Of course, getting a new job is not a straightforward process and will require time and effort on your part—we'll look more specifically at that process later on in this chapter—but the question you have to ask yourself is: Are you willing to put in that effort? If you're serious about optimizing your career for salary, then the answer is probably going to be yes.

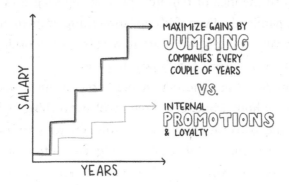

TIME, BENEFITS, AND PERSONAL GROWTH

As I mentioned earlier in this chapter, there are of course other reasons beyond pay that you might want to focus on employed work. In addition to security, these include the various benefits and opportunities for growth that can be achieved by being part of a company, as well as the ability to rely on defined working hours. There are going to be variations to these, of course, depending on the job you go for, so in this section I want to spend a little time looking at these features when considering jobs as we continue to think about the objectives for which we're optimizing. It's also important to bear in mind that, even if particular benefits or arrangements are not advertised as being part of a job, there's no harm in asking if the company is willing to be flexible on those points. Remember: always be on offense.

When it comes to time and flexibility, this can be a key concern with regard to job selection. Some jobs might require you to relocate, so you'll have to ask yourself whether that's something you're willing to do. On the other hand, if it's not something you'd want to consider, you might be able to explore whether a remote working arrangement might be possible. The one thing that has really changed in the world of employment following COVID-19 is that companies are now a lot more open to the idea of remote work, having seen how it worked during the pandemic. Even if it's not something immediately offered by the company, you can always ask to see if remote working is on the table. You may be surprised at how often it is.

Working hours are another element you'll want to look at. The standard forty-hour workweek often involves working eight hours a day, from nine to five, five days a week. Now, if that works for you, then fine, there's no problem. But again, you might want to explore alternatives, either because you have other commitments, such as childcare or other family concerns, or simply because you'd prefer a different arrangement. One increasingly common setup is the 10/4 working week—that's where you work for ten hours a day instead of eight, and then for only four days a week, taking Friday off. It amounts to the same number of hours in total, but then it does mean that you have a longer weekend at your disposal. Or you could aim to work nine hours a day and have every other Friday off. These are all flexible alternatives to the standard forty-hour week, and again, though companies may not be offering these arrangements right off the bat, there's no harm in asking whether it's something they'd consider.

And, of course, benefits such as paid time off, sick leave, health insurance, and possible parental leave are all other elements to consider when looking for particular jobs. The important thing is to establish what is important to you and make sure that those points are what you take into consideration in the process of looking for a job, whether that's by targeting jobs that offer those benefits or by asking potential employers for precisely what you want.

The other benefit that comes with employed work is that of personal development and growth, and this can be quite a tricky one to pin down. Of course, as hackers we're all about personal growth—remember the hacker characteristic of constant improvement—but exactly how this is achieved in a particular job isn't always clear. Employers are always very quick to list the various opportunities for learning and development that their jobs will provide, but, as usual, what the employers are really interested in is the labor their employees will provide to the company rather than the benefits the employees will receive, and because, unlike pay, growth opportunities are not quantifiable, there's no formal way to hold employers to account with regard to such promises. As such, it's up to you to determine the opportunities for personal development and keep track of them.

A good way to do this is to write a resumé of your future self—project yourself three years into the future and write out a resumé listing all the skills you should have as someone who has worked in the particular role and for that company for three years. Are those skills you'd want to develop? If not, then perhaps the job isn't for you, or at least it's not going to provide you with the personal development you want. If they are skills you want to develop, then it will be up to you to keep track of whether you're actually developing them. Keep tabs on yourself—go back to your future resumé and ask yourself how close you are to being that person. If after a year or so you're no closer, then perhaps the job isn't providing you with the opportunities you thought it would, and it's time to look for an alternative.

GETTING A JOB

As I've said throughout this chapter, you have to be clear on what you're optimizing for from the outset. Is it salary, job title, flexibility, benefits, personal growth, or a combination of more than one of these? You should also consider what kind of a company you want to work for. The experience of working within a large corporate environment is radically different from that of working within a small startup. In a smaller company you're likely to have a broader scope and be expected to take on a wide variety of duties, as there probably aren't going to be enough people on the team for everyone to be specialized. On the other hand, in a larger organization there will be that capacity for specialization and as such you'd likely be looking at a role where you'll have more specific duties. Consider all these factors and the hierarchy of what's most important to you and what you're willing to compromise on and you'll be in the optimal position to start applying for jobs.

Having determined your objectives, it's time to move on to the next step of the hacker methodology, and in the case of getting a job it's about doing reconnaissance when applying for jobs.

The application process itself can be quite grueling, but by applying the hacker mindset you can maximize your chances of being successful. If you're applying to a large corporation, you may encounter situations where the first step companies take is to use artificial intelligence to filter out resumés that don't contain certain key words. What these key words are will vary from sector to sector and role to role, but a little research will help you find what you need to include. Of course, this only gets you past the first stage, and there are many more ways in which you can optimize your applications for success.

Applying the hacker methodology in the job application process can pay serious dividends. I know it can be very tempting to use generic resumés and cover letters when applying for jobs, sending in what is essentially the same application to as many companies as possible and seeing what sticks. However, this isn't likely to be a very successful approach and it's emblematic of the slacker mindset, since it's all execution with no planning. As a hacker, don't underestimate the importance of the reconnaissance and analysis stages of the methodology. You need to find out everything you can, not just about the role you're applying for but about the broader company as well. Look at the job descriptions of similar jobs within the same company. You might also want to look on LinkedIn or elsewhere for the resumés of people who are on the team. Look for the commonalities in terms of skills that the company values, but also look for the gaps where the company may be missing out on particular skills or abilities. You can then tailor your application to show how you can fill those gaps while also having the requisite skills to fill the role. The key point to remember here is that tailoring your application will massively increase your chances of success, and the best way to do that is with hacker-level reconnaissance and analysis.

In terms of how you present your skills, you can think of it as a T-structure—this is where you demonstrate a substantial level of skill in one area (the I of the T) while also showcasing a breadth of other skills (the – of the T), which is where you show you bring additional value to the company. There is a phrase you might have come across: a jack of all trades, master of none. This describes someone who has a wide variety of skills but isn't really specialized in any one particular area. Being a jack of all trades isn't a great strategy when it comes to looking for a job, because hirers are often looking for someone who has a great depth of expertise in the area most relevant to the job. On the other hand, no one can be a total expert in all kinds of different fields, which is why the T-structure forms the best balance, showing deep expertise in one area with a broad range of ancillary skills supporting that area of expertise. This is actually how most computer hackers are, as they often need a broad understanding of a variety of technological platforms, while making use of deeper expertise in a few specific areas. Presenting yourself in the same way when applying for jobs will also pay dividends. Take this approach and you'll come across as a substantially more attractive potential hire as compared with others.

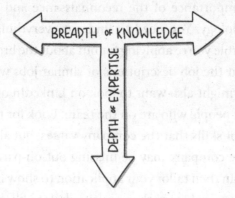

Another way to gain advantage is to have informal interviews with current employees within the relevant department or team. This simply means getting in touch with those employees and asking to speak to them as a potential applicant, asking them about what it's like to work at the company. This will obviously give you further insight into the company and its values, which will help you in putting together your application, but it could also help you stand out from other applicants as someone who is particularly motivated to join the company, giving you an edge against other applicants. With some subtle questioning you can also get insights into the particularities of the hiring managers and whoever else is likely to interview you once your application is accepted. There are a variety of questions you can ask to get the insights you'd be looking for. For example: Am I replacing someone or is this a new role? If the former, what did that person bring to the team that made it work? What does success look like for this position? Where are the gaps in the skills of the current team's makeup? What are some of the challenges facing the team at the moment? I'm sure you can see how the answers to some of these questions will give an advantage in the interview with the hiring manager, since you'll be able to portray yourself as someone who perfectly fills the gaps and requirements in the team as it is.

Doing this reconnaissance and analysis will put you in the ideal position to execute your application. You'll also want to make use of the hacker principle of living off the land at this point. You'll be able to find typical interview questions online, and you can discover more about the company itself and its structure on websites such as Glassdoor and LinkedIn. Using the information you've gathered will maximize the chances of your application being taken forward to the interview stage, and you'll find that the information you used to tailor your application is the same information that will be useful during the interview. Familiarity with the company and its culture will be key to demonstrating your suitability for the role, and showing that you possess not only the skills required for the role but also broader skills that add extra value (skills that fill those gaps you identified earlier) will differentiate you from other applicants and give you a distinct advantage.

And, of course, don't forget the execution stage of the methodology. It might sound pretty obvious, but applying for jobs can be a very grueling process, particularly if you live in a big city with lots of competition. Having done your reconnaissance and analysis, you'll need to have the persistence to put your plan into action and work through those applications.

REASSESS

Of course, this final stage of the hacker methodology is the linchpin of the whole process and it's what's most important when it comes to making sure you don't get stuck in a rut. Once you've got the job you were after, the job that fulfills all the objectives you established at the beginning, you should regularly take a step back and look at how things are going. Are you where you wanted to be? Have things turned out differently than you expected? Have your circumstances changed, whereby you have new priorities and therefore new objectives? Reassessing the situation and then going back to the beginning of the hacker methodology will help ensure that you're constantly keeping your career on track and achieving what you want to achieve.

Applying the hacker mindset to your career isn't just about making sure you're successful in that one job application or that you manage to get that particular promotion—it's about ensuring that your career is always either precisely where you want it to be or moving toward where you want it to be. Following the hacker methodology in its entirety, from establishing your objectives through to the stage of reassessment and then back to the objectives, is how to ensure that your career is fulfilling not just for a moment but in perpetuity.

Chapter 12

ENTREPRENEURSHIP

×

HACKER MINDSET

Working as an employee is certainly the right answer for some people, but for others it will never really tick all the boxes of living a satisfying and fulfilling life. That was certainly the case for me, and my solution was to start my own business.

As I've mentioned earlier in this book, for most of my employed life I was working as a cybersecurity expert at various government organizations, and it was while I was working at the Federal Reserve Bank that the limits of being an employee really began to irk me. Promotions were scarce, and even when I did get them, the increase in my pay wasn't that great. On top of that, though the work I was doing was certainly interesting, it was the same sort of thing day in, day out, and it had begun to feel monotonous. More and more I felt that all the advantages of being an employee (job security, clearly defined work hours, etc.) were not enough to make up for the disadvantages. That's when I began to look for alternatives.

While working as an ethical hacker I'd always been frustrated at the difficulty we had in sourcing necessary equipment from various suppliers. We'd have to look all over the place to find the bits of equipment that we needed, and there was always a possibility that the particular gadget we'd ordered would end up not working. *Wouldn't it be great*, I'd often say to myself, *if there were one place that sourced all this stuff and had user reviews so we'd know how good it was?* Even when I was still a solid Monday-to-Friday employee I'd identified a gap in the market, and when it came time to look for a way out, it was an obvious decision to fill that gap by starting my own business. Even before consciously realizing it, I'd been applying the hacker mindset to my own life.

I didn't immediately quit my job and start the business, though. I knew that turning an idea into a successful business wasn't a sure thing, and putting all my eggs into the business basket from the outset didn't suit my risk appetite. At first I began to work on building up the business in my spare time while still working as an employee full-time. It was a slow process because I didn't have a huge amount of time to dedicate to it, but after a few months I saw that the business was beginning to gain some traction. I became a little more confident and made the decision to go part-time at the Federal Reserve, working there for only three days a week, leaving me with the remaining four days a week to dedicate to working on my business. The income I continued to get from my day job, even though it was reduced due to my going part-time, allowed me to sustain my life as I worked on making the business more profitable. The business steadily grew and eventually I decided to exhibit it at DEF CON, the world's largest and most iconic hacker convention. I spent $10,000, my entire savings at that point, in stocking up, and packed up and went to Las Vegas, where the convention was being held. It was a three-day convention, and in less than three hours after setting up on the first day, I'd sold out my entire inventory and generated a nice profit on that $10,000 investment. Of course, at the time I was kicking myself, thinking I should have bought a lot more stock on credit, but hindsight always makes things obvious. At the time, I took a risk that I was comfortable with.

The money I brought in at DEF CON was certainly good, but the real benefit of exhibiting there was that it showed me this was a really strong and viable business. At that point I quit my job at the Federal Reserve completely and began to focus on the business full-time, and the rest is history. Pretty quickly I'd turned what had begun as just an idea I had while working as an employee into a seven-figure business. Should I have done it all sooner? Of course—like I said, hindsight is always 20/20—but at the time I had to think about the risks, and I made the appropriate decisions based on the risks that I was willing to take. Being realistic is of course a key characteristic of the hacker mindset and that meant being realistic about the risks of starting a new business.

IT'S NOT EASY BEING AN ENTREPRENEUR . . .

So, being realistic, let's take a look at some of the challenges of starting a business.

The first thing we have to make clear is that having a great idea or thesis for a business is by no means a guarantee that that business becomes a success. Recent statistics on this are quite stark—they show that of all the startups in the United States, 18 percent fail within the first year, 50 percent fail within the first five years, and 65 percent fail within the first ten years. Obviously, these statistics take in *all* startups, and as I'm sure you'll be thinking, not all business ideas are created equal. We've all seen those episodes of *Shark Tank* where hapless wannabes turn up with the most insane ideas, expecting big investments. They all get laughed out of the studio, but they also all count as startups and must be contributing to these statistics of business failures. However, that's not to say that the only businesses that fail are those that are based on bad ideas; many startups that at first look to be based on a solid business plan end up failing, too, and that can be for a variety of reasons, such as lack of investment, lack of development, or just plain bad luck. Of course, many of these failed entrepreneurs will not have been applying the hacker mindset to their businesses, and applying the hacker mindset is a great way of maximizing your chances of success, but it remains the case that starting a new business always involves a certain amount of risk. In my own case, I decided to offset that risk by continuing as an employee part-time until I felt confident that my business was probably going to be a success, but for any budding entrepreneur, facing the risk of possible failure is a hurdle that has to be surmounted, one way or another.

The second point to make here is that being a business owner requires a lot of hard work, particularly at the beginning when you're first building up your business. Many new entrepreneurs find themselves in a situation where they are bootstrapping, which means they're trying to start a company with little capital and no outside investment, having to rely on their own resources and time to build their businesses in the early stages. It's not easy and requires a lot of discipline. Unlike being an employee, there's no one telling you when you start or finish work, or making sure that you work a certain number of hours in a week. How much time you're going to spend working on it is completely up to you, and you need to have the discipline and self-motivation to make sure you're doing what needs to be done when it needs to be done. You'll also have to undertake multiple roles in the early stages of your business. Most large corporations have different levels of personnel to fulfill different roles—they have the executives at the top who develop the overall vision for the company, then beneath them are the managers who strategize and create plans to effectively implement the vision, then beneath them are the workers who execute the managers' plans and deliver the product or service that the company provides. With your own startup you're going to have to take on all these roles, from working out the overall vision and strategy of the business right down to the most menial tasks such as addressing envelopes or loading a truck.

Following from this, another thing to consider is that it can be quite easy to become lost or overwhelmed in the sheer volume and variety of things you need to be on top of. Building your startup will certainly eat into your free time. Remember when I said I went part-time with my day job to spend more time building up my business? I worked three days a week working for the Federal Reserve, and then four days a week working on my business—which is, of course, a total of seven days a week of work, and I've no doubt that if I'd quit the day job altogether at that point, I'd have worked seven days a week on my business. That's just the way startup goes—there are always more things to do than there is time to do them, and the business will begin to monopolize your attention. And there'll be no one there to tell you to stop or to pay you overtime—as I said earlier, it'll come down to your own discipline and self-control. Similarly, if you end up taking the business in the wrong direction, there'll be no one there to tell you not to. When you're doing everything yourself, it can be relatively easy to fall down a rabbit hole that leads to nowhere and to lose sight of the overall picture. Here, the hacker mindset can help—never forget the pendulum that represents the approach a hacker takes, balancing planning and execution perfectly. When you're putting all your time and effort into your own startup, it can be all too easy to fall into the trap of focusing too much on execution. You need to make sure that you're stepping back to look at the bigger picture and keep on top of the planning side of things as well.

Finally, I just want to add that building a business is never a case of instant success. Hardly any businesses are profitable as soon as they start. In fact, they usually suffer losses at the beginning, and it almost always takes a little while before they break even and then begin to bring in a profit. As such, it will probably take a few years before you start to see a return on all the time, effort, and capital you've put into the business. You have to be in it for the long haul if you're going to make a success out of it.

...BUT IT CAN BE WORTH IT!

Owning a business is certainly a challenge, there's no denying that, but it can also be a wonderful experience. Some of the most fulfilled people I know are entrepreneurs, myself included. Being an independent business owner comes with some great benefits, and the first is just that: you're independent. Though I talked about the lack of any oversight or guidance as a negative earlier on, being your own boss can also be tremendously freeing. You're in the driver's seat and you get to decide how things are going to be. If you are currently or were recently an employee, you might have on occasion become frustrated with the decisions made by the company's executive board. Sometimes those business decisions just make no sense and you can clearly see what the problems are and how they might be addressed, but you're not the one who makes those decisions. Owning your own business means you can make those decisions for yourself and nobody can counter.

Being an independent business owner also means you have the flexibility to determine your own working style. It's up to you to decide precisely when and where you work. You want to take the next Wednesday off just because, or you want to go on that impromptu holiday starting tomorrow? Sure, no problem—there's no overbearing manager around to complain that you should have put in your leave request three months earlier. Similarly, perhaps you prefer to work from home, or from a café, or from an office, or even from a beach in the Bahamas as you travel around the Caribbean. It's all up to you. There's no company policy insisting that you show up to the office a certain number of days a week, or a disapproving executive asking why you're still in your pajamas during a Zoom call. If you want to spend the day working from home in just your pajamas, then you can do that—there's no one to stop you.

Of course, I have to add to this that all these decisions will have an impact on your business. You can't choose to work one day a week and then wonder why your fledgling business isn't growing at the rate you'd like it to. And it may be that you actually do work more efficiently in an office as opposed to working from home. Much can even be said on the subject of sartorial psychology. I once knew someone who would get dressed up in a full suit, right down to formal shoes, every time he was going to phone a tricky client. The client couldn't see him, but he felt that the suit gave him more authority and helped him deal with such clients more robustly. Every decision has its consequences, but it's also the case that what is the right decision for some is not the right decision for others. The advantage of being a business owner is that you can determine exactly what kind of working style works for you and for your business and do it, as opposed to the one-size-fits-all approach taken by most companies to their employees.

Another huge advantage to being an entrepreneur is the potential for much greater income growth as compared with employed work. Usually corporate wages don't keep up with the rate of inflation—this is quite a notable trend, particularly as businesses are often quick to raise their prices in relation to rising costs. This goes back to the point I made in the previous chapter, that corporations are interested only in maximizing profits, and one aspect of that is keeping wages of employees as low as possible. However, as a business owner, your wages are in your own hands. If the Consumer Price Index goes up, you can make sure that the money you're personally taking home goes up to match that.

More broadly, owning a successful business will almost always mean that your income will far outpace what you would have been earning as an employee. This was certainly the case for me. After a few years of building up my business, my income had become substantially more than what the most senior staff were earning at my previous workplace; and compared with the incomes of some of my peers who had moved on to executive roles—well, let's just say I have no regrets about leaving all that behind. Again, this isn't to say that starting your own business automatically means you'll be taking in a huge income. Bear in mind that word I used in the first sentence of this paragraph: "owning a *successful* business." What being an entre-·preneur does is change the equation of how your income is determined. As an employee your wages are constrained by the parameters of conventional career progression. As a business owner your income can balloon very quickly if you grow your business properly and make the right decisions. As with everything else, the power is in your hands.

Of course, I should also talk about the corollary to having a highly varied workload as a business owner. Yes, it can be daunting to be faced with such a broad range of responsibilities, but the flip side is that you'll have the opportunity to do all kinds of different things. Employees are often pigeonholed inside the parameters of their jobs and are rarely afforded the chance of broadening their horizons. For example, if you're employed as a number cruncher you probably won't have the opportunity to explore being very creative, or if your job is to fulfill a very specific role as part of the wider business, you won't have the opportunity to design a more all-encompassing plan. As a business owner you'll be able to do all these things—the opportunities for building your skills in any area you can imagine are boundless.

Finally, I just want to say that owning and growing a business can be a really rewarding experience. It's your business, you're fully in control of all the decisions, and when it becomes successful you'll know that that's all down to you. There's a tremendous feeling of satisfaction in knowing you've created something and built it to a point where it's successful. I have a friend who's a novelist and he once told me that whenever he's feeling a bit down, he gets all the books that he's published and piles them up on the table, looks at them, and thinks, *I've accomplished that*, and it lifts his spirits. It's the same as a business owner—having that sense of accomplishment and knowing you've put in the effort, made the right decisions, and created a successful business can be a really uplifting feeling.

If reading through this fills you with excitement and eagerness, perhaps starting a business is the right thing for you!

BUSINESS OBJECTIVES

As with everything else, when applying the hacker methodology it's important to establish what your objectives are from the outset. What precisely is it that you want to optimize for when you set out to become an entrepreneur? This will inform your approach, as well as the type of business you can build.

Obviously, the first thing you might want to think about is optimizing your strategy for money. There's no doubt that you'll be wanting to make money as a business owner, but it's not so simple as just leaving it there. How much money do you want to make, and how quickly? Do you want enough money to simply pay the bills and live comfortably? Or is it more important for you to be able to live a more lavish lifestyle, spending money on expensive items without even worrying about it? I'm sure you're all reading this thinking that of course you'd want to make more money than less, but if maximizing your income to such a high degree is a primary objective for you, it may be that you'll have to compromise on some of the other objectives.

For example, many budding entrepreneurs view themselves as striving to become the owners of the next unicorn—the next startup business with a valuation of over $1 billion. But the fact of the matter is that unicorns are few and far between and to become the owner of one not only requires a huge amount of hard work, it also requires a huge degree of good fortune. This is where analyzing your objectives when it comes to making money comes in. Is building a billion-dollar company as quickly as possible really the most important thing to you? If so, then you can certainly go for it, but also be aware that you'll be making sacrifices when it comes to other choices around the business. But if—as is going to be the case for the vast majority of people—making *that* much money off the bat is not the be-all and end-all of things, you'd probably be better off trying to build up what I like to call a cash camel. A cash camel is like a cash cow—that is, a business that doesn't require a huge amount of money to get started and will reliably generate a nice amount of profit—but a cash camel will also have a healthy amount of cash in reserve for added security. That's less "amazing" than building a unicorn, but it's certainly a hell of a lot more reliable. Codie Sanchez often talks about this kind of approach—she's an investor who embraces a "contrarian" approach to investing, and she frequently makes the point that modestly successful businesses are still successful, and are a lot more achievable than building a business that takes in billions of dollars.

Another thing you'll want to assess when considering objectives is time and flexibility. As I mentioned earlier, a big advantage of being an independent business owner is the ability to set your own hours and working conditions, but again, doing this will have an impact on the kind of business you can build. For example, a business whereby you are personally providing a service such as being a consultant or a tutor will necessarily exert a high demand on your time, though it would also give you quite a high income from the outset. On the other hand, an ecommerce business would require a lot of time to start up, but as you develop it and the business becomes more stable and self-contained, the demand on your time would become substantially reduced. Granted, it would take a little longer to get the business to a stage where it's bringing in as much income as you would be doing working as a consultant.

Similarly, your working environment is a factor to bear in mind when deciding how to go about starting your own business. There are many businesses that can be operated remotely. In fact, this is a major factor driving many people who want to live a nomadic life, moving from one place to another, while they run their online businesses. If flexibility around where you work from is an important objective for you, then operating a business that's completely online may be the best option for you.

Some people are motivated to become business owners because of the status and prestige that comes with being a successful entrepreneur. I would suggest being wary of such motivations. An example of someone who was motivated purely by prestige is Anna Sorokin, whom I referred to earlier in this book. She wanted to be recognized for having a glamorous lifestyle and to be respected as the founder of what she rather narcissistically called the Anna Delvey Foundation, but ultimately she had nothing else to back it up and she ended up being convicted of fraud and going to jail. Another, rather more high-profile, example would be that of Elizabeth Holmes. She was the founder of Theranos, a health technology company that claimed to be able to carry out blood tests using very small amounts of blood. It seemed to be a very successful venture, obtaining a valuation of around $10 billion at its peak—the only problem was that the claims about the blood tests turned out to be completely false, and Elizabeth Holmes also ended up being convicted of fraud. Status and prestige are things that will come with being successful, but if you make obtaining them your primary goal, you may find yourself in danger of missing out not only on the prestige but also on the success in the longer term.

The alternative to being driven by status is being driven by social impact. It may not all be personal gain for you—it may be the case that you want to make sure that your business achieves some kind of social good. Now, it could be that your business by its very nature has a social impact—there are plenty of businesses that work toward bettering the lives of underprivileged people—but if it doesn't, you can still make this an objective. You could, for example, resolve to donate 1 percent of the profits of your business to charity, or 5 percent, or even 10 percent.

Many successful companies were founded on such principles. To take one example, let's have a look at Bombas. Bombas is a clothes company that was founded with the intention of being successful commercially while making a real impact helping people in homeless shelters. The item that is requested by homeless shelters more than any other is socks, so Bombas started off selling socks with a "one purchased, one donated" policy, whereby for every pair of socks purchased by customers, the company would donate a pair of socks to homeless shelters. As the company grew more successful, it expanded into the second- and third-most-requested items by homeless shelters—namely, underwear and shirts—continuing to donate these items of clothing for every one purchased.

And this is just one example of how a business can operate while working to bring about social change. When it comes to your business, you can organize it to work toward literally any cause you want. Remember, it's your business, so it's your choice. The important thing here, as it is with all the types of objectives, is to be clear on what it is you're working toward from the outset.

WHAT'S THE RIGHT BUSINESS FOR YOU?

With your objectives established, it's time to work out what kind of business would work best to serve those objectives. It can be a bit tricky to balance all your objectives and figure out how best they can be achieved through a business, but thankfully there's a process that can help clarify that.

The Japanese concept of *ikigai* can be helpful here. The word *ikigai* can roughly be translated as "reason for being," and it refers to those projects or endeavors that bring meaning or value to one's life. The way by which you can discover your *ikigai* is what is particularly pertinent here. The idea is to list ideas and determine whether they fall into any of four categories: (1) What you love; (2) What the world needs; (3) What you can be paid for; and (4) What you are good at. Ideas that fall into several of these categories can be identified accordingly. For example, an endeavor that you are good at and that you can be paid for would be a profession, an endeavor that you love and you are good at would be a passion, and an endeavor that you love and that the world needs would be a mission. Something that fits all four categories, lying at the heart of the Venn diagram, is your *ikigai*.

When I set out to be an entrepreneur, I took a similar approach in working out the best business venture for my objectives. I didn't use the same categories as those used in determining one's *ikigai*; instead, I listed the various factors that related to my objectives, from both an input and an output perspective, and then drew a matrix on a sheet of paper whereby I could see how well each business idea scored against each of these factors. Ideally I was looking for something that required minimal input in the long run and that gave maximum output, which of course is pretty much the definition of a smart investment. Putting all that down on paper like this helped me to see more clearly what kind of business would work best for me. In terms of input, I considered the amount of time I'd need to put in, the amount of money I'd need to invest, and the complexity of the route to success. On the output side I considered the amount of money I was likely to make, whether the idea had multiple leverage points for further opportunities, and to what degree the idea could be outsourceable so that it would become a self-sustaining system. I didn't go into great detail on all these factors. For example, when it came to estimating the money in and the money out, I was content to go for $, $$, $$$—after all, the purpose of the matrix was not to form a full business plan; it was only to identify which business ideas were most likely to allow me to realize my objectives.

BUSINESS ANALYSIS WORKSHEET

BUSINESS		INPUTS			OUTPUTS			DECISION
IDEA/ PROJECT	TYPE/ CATEGORY	TIME	$ SPENT	COMPLEXITY	$ PROJECTION (AUDIENCE SIZE × PRICE)	MULTIPLE LEVERAGE OPPORTUNITIES?	LONG-TERM OUTSOURCE/ PASSIVE?	NEXT ACTIONS?

As it turned out, ecommerce was the answer I was looking for. It had small overheads and so it was relatively easy to start making a profit early on, it was scalable, and once I had the business established, a lot of the actual mechanics of it could be outsourced, allowing the business to sustain itself with minimal time investment from myself in the longer term. This was the right choice for me and it ticked all the boxes I'd set out as part of my objectives. Determining what works best for you is as simple as following that same process. Just remember that there are all kinds of business opportunities out there, whether it's selling digital products or selling physical products, providing a service such as coaching or consulting or even dog walking, producing content on YouTube or podcasts, or even opening up a brick-and-mortar bakery—any of these and many, many more could be the right solution for you. The thing to do is to consider all the possibilities, see how they stack up against the various factors you've identified, and settle on the one that most fulfills your objectives.

RECONNAISSANCE

A further element to working out the best type of business to start can come at the reconnaissance stage. There's so much information out there about various businesses, particularly the more successful ones, in terms of their revenue and their spending, overall profits, and so on. The internet is full of resources to find this kind of information. For example, the website Crunchbase allows you to search for any public company you please, and it will provide you with some of this data. More broadly, some smart searching on the major search engines will get you even more information. It's almost as if these companies, just by doing what they do, are providing you with a road map of how to be a successful business. Of course, with great success comes great competition, and many of the most successful businesses quickly find themselves having to compete against other companies that think they can do the same thing but better.

I have a few friends who specifically *don't* want their businesses to make their way onto the Fortune 500 list, specifically because they know that that added exposure will lead to a lot more competition. From the perspective of a budding entrepreneur, however, this can provide some great opportunities. Let's say there's a successful business operating in an area that you're already familiar with, and you thoroughly study how that company operates. You see a gap in their processes and you identify a way to operate that kind of business 1 percent better—there's your edge to outcompete them. The world of business can be ruthless, and being ruthlessly competitive can be one path to success. Remembering the first hacker principle we looked at—be on offense—in cases such as these can be the difference between success and failure.

There are also many resources available you can take advantage of, particularly online. Remember Hacker Principle 3: Living Off the Land—be resourceful and make full use of whatever is easily available. Considering this, certain types of businesses will present themselves more readily to you. For example, in the product and direct-to-consumer space you might want to take advantage of Amazon's Fulfillment by Amazon (FBA) scheme, whereby you can outsource the fulfillment of orders to Amazon, so that they pick up and deliver whatever you're selling. Of course, this isn't free, but the fact that you're taking advantage of Amazon's already well-established delivery infrastructure means that your overheads will be substantially reduced. In fact, generally speaking, Amazon is a good platform for product retailers because it's so ubiquitous. People are so used to buying things online these days and particularly from Amazon that they hardly ever shop around or compare prices with other platforms. Amazon has a little bit of a monopoly at the moment when it comes to online retail, and though that's probably not great for competition in general, it is something you can take advantage of.

If you pair the outsourcing of the delivery of products with the outsourcing of the production of products, then you arrive at the concept of drop shipping. This is where you're selling products, but the entire supply chain is outsourced, which means you can operate the entire business remotely, and once it's suitably established you can easily transition the business to something that is self-sustaining, requiring minimal input from yourself as the owner to keep it going. This concept can also be applied to more creative business ideas—for example, print-on-demand services have become a lot more viable in recent times thanks to the advancement of technology. Whether it's clothing, or decor, or books, or a range of other options, all you have to do is design the product and then take advantage of the existing services and infrastructure to have that product delivered to customers.

These are just a few examples of the kind of businesses that have been more enabled thanks to resources available through the internet and thanks to technology. Ultimately, it's up to you to determine what kind of business works best for you and your objectives. Doing your reconnaissance and working through the analysis step of the hacker methodology will be vital in figuring out precisely what this is, and once that's worked out it's up to you to execute and put those findings into action.

REASSESS

Finally, let's consider how the last stage of the hacker methodology is realized in the context of business.

It may very well be the case that, having decided on the type of business that's best for you, having done your reconnaissance and analysis, having developed your business plan and set out to execute that plan, you find that things haven't gone quite the way you'd anticipated. It may even be that your business isn't succeeding where you thought it would. Remember, a business is a system, and working out the various parts of a system and how they can be overcome is what the hacker mindset is all about. This is where the hacker principle of pivoting comes to the fore. You need to step back and ask yourself how things might be changed. Was it not the right product? Perhaps there are some tweaks that could be made to make the product more viable. Or you might want to ask yourself whether the particular solution to the problem you'd originally identified was the right kind of solution for the market. Maybe you could change how that solution works so that it fits the market better.

It could have been the wrong product for the market (product-market fit), but equally it could have been the wrong product for the available platforms (product-platform fit), or even for yourself (product-founder fit). On the market side, it may be that the way in which you've tried to solve a problem that people have, or to fill a gap in people's wants, didn't quite work. From a platform perspective, it's important to recognize that you don't control the major channels through which your product is going to reach people, such as Google, X, or other platforms. They set the rules in terms of what's going to reach people, so you have to make sure that your product fits into those rules. And as far as the product being the right fit for you goes, you might have discovered a gap in the market and worked out how to fill it, but if it's not something you can believe in and be passionate about, your chances of success are going to be low. Taking a step back and looking at how things might be improved is crucial to making things work out.

The recursive nature of the hacker methodology is what gives it its power. It gives you the opportunity to go back into the reconnaissance and analysis stages, to use what you've learned to further inform and alter your strategy and maximize your chances of success. And even if you come to the conclusion that the business is just not going to work out, remember that the hacker principle of pivoting means that you can make the most out of failure. Even if you haven't achieved your objectives, you'll have learned more and will have more leverage points for your next set of objectives.

And even if the business has been successful, you still need to reassess. Remember the pendulum that represents the hacker mindset—even if you're being successful you don't want to get stuck on execution, as that will likely lead to complacency and stagnation. You always want to be going back and forth between planning and execution. Yes, you've developed a successful business, but is that the end of it all? It may be the case that, having achieved success in your business, your objectives will change. Perhaps you'll want to drastically expand your business, or maybe you'll want to branch off into a different venture. It might even be the case that you'll want to sell your business for a healthy sum, invest that money so that you have a nice and reliable passive income, and go on to live a life of leisure—more on that in the next chapter! Ultimately, the hacker mindset is about not only achieving one set of goals, but also ensuring that you're continuously making sure your life is where you want it to be, wherever that may be.

Chapter 13

PERSONAL FINANCE

✖

HACKER MINDSET

When it comes to thinking about investing money and managing personal finances, you could do a lot worse than taking Warren Buffett as an example. Largely recognized as one of the best, if not *the* best, investors in the world, the man has amassed a vast fortune by way of shrewd investments and a pretty successful overarching investment philosophy. Now, I'm not saying that everyone can achieve Warren Buffett levels of financial success—obviously, if everyone were to become a multibillionaire, inflation would go through the roof—but as we'll see a little later on, there are some basic principles that significantly contributed to his success that can be applied by anyone who's managing their personal finances. Of course, Warren Buffett is not a hacker, but, as we will see, his approach, and that of many successful investors and finance managers, demonstrates some key aspects of the hacker mindset.

HOW MUCH IS ENOUGH?

The first thing to think of when you start to consider the subject of personal finances and independent wealth is precisely how much money you need. This is probably the most important question to ask at the objectives stage when applying the hacker methodology to finances, and being clear on this is crucial to determining your overall strategy, so that's what we're going to focus on to begin with.

Many of us fall into the trap of assuming that the money we're taking in from our jobs or even our businesses is a lot because it's a larger amount than our parents earned when we were kids. It's pretty natural to use one's parents as a baseline—after all, they are our main point of reference when we're growing up, and more often than not it's our parents who set our expectations in life. However, the fact is that things change and the environment within which our parents and their generation could succeed is not the same as the one we find ourselves in now. I'm sure we've all seen those memes online of baby boomers telling millennials that it's really easy to buy a house—all they need to do is work hard, save up, and stop spending so much money on smashed avocado. They're a good laugh, but they do also underline a serious point, which is that the approach that might have worked when you could buy a house for $50,000 isn't going to work when houses now cost over $400,000. With inflation and the general rise in the cost of living over the years, what might feel like a lot of money in our heads actually doesn't leave us with that much spending power.

This isn't a gospel of despair—on the contrary, I'm here to show you how to make things work, but we first have to recognize that the approach of working hard, earning a "decent" amount, and saving up just isn't going to cut it in the current environment. There is another way, however, and that's where the hacker mindset comes into play. Applying the hacker mindset to managing your finances will allow you to supplement, and possibly eventually replace, the money you receive from your work or business endeavors with a reliable stream of income.

As always, it would be best to start off by adopting a realistic approach and thinking about some of the positives and negatives when it comes to taking an active role in money management. Happily, there's not a great deal to go into on this as, when it comes down to it, using money to make money is a pretty straightforward process.

First, I have to say that the process of successful management of personal finances requires a good deal of patience. There is no magic formula that will turn an investment of $100 to $1 million overnight. That's not to say that these massive gains on investments don't happen—they do—but more often than not they rely more on a huge amount of luck than anything else, and that's not the kind of thing you can rely on. In reality, a successful long-term investment strategy involves working out your plan at the beginning and then a lot of waiting while your profits build up, with perhaps the odd tweak here or there. The other side of this coin is the need for discipline. It can be very easy to be tempted by the large potential gains to be made by day-trading on the stock exchange, particularly if some of your contemporaries are bragging about the huge profits they've made trading stocks. Of course, they're much more likely to brag about their wins than publicize their losses, and the fact is that in the long term you're almost always better off sticking with a sensible (if not terribly exciting) plan.

The positive side of this is that the whole process is not very difficult. The whole thing really comes down to pretty straightforward math, and once you've got that sorted you can just rely on the system to work for you. There's no need to worry or to have to make constant decisions—that's all taken care of. You might need to make occasional tweaks and adjustments, most particularly if your objectives evolve, but beyond that you can basically sit back and relax. Take care of the preparations and the rest will take care of itself. Ultimately, your investments will take care of you.

YOU NEED MONEY TO MAKE MONEY

When it comes to considering objectives for personal finances, the most obvious is optimizing for money. You might think money is the *only* objective with regard to managing personal finances, but there are a few others we will look at soon. Money is, however, going to be at the heart of it and it's the first objective we're going to look at. In particular at this point, I want to talk a bit about how you need to have some initial capital to make the finance management work for you in the long run. Unless you're the sudden recipient of a very large inheritance, most of your capital is going to come from your work income, either as an employee or as a business owner. I've already spoken about how to maximize your income in both of those contexts in the previous two chapters, but there are certainly a few more general points to be made.

The first is that it's often easier to earn more than to spend less. If you're accustomed to spending money on particular luxuries, it's often very difficult to break this habit. I mean, you could if you were really determined to do so, but nine times out of ten it's easier to earn more money while maintaining your spending habits. Of course, you could and should use the hacker methodology to improve your income as we talked about in the previous chapters, but you might also want to look at the possibility of developing multiple income streams. Are there sources of income you can take advantage of other than your main job? Is there a side hustle you can do to bring in a few extra dollars? These options are certainly something to consider.

There is also a wealth of optimizations you can make to your day-to-day life that will help maximize your income. For example, you can take advantage of cash-back and rewards schemes offered by credit card companies. Many people associate buying things on credit with being broke, but that's far from the truth. Using credit cards when you don't *need* them is actually a pretty smart strategy, as long as you make sure to pay off the full balance of your credit cards every month so you won't have to pay any interest, while still reaping the rewards—5 percent cash back here, 4 percent there—it all adds up. And there are opportunities for saving all over the place. For example, if you spend a certain amount of money at Costco, they'll give you a discount on the gas that they sell. Of course, this doesn't mean that you go to Costco and spend loads of money in order to get the discount, but if you take advantage of that discount in the normal course of doing your grocery shopping, that savings you'll make on the discounts will begin to add up.

You might also consider the possibility of geographic arbitrage—this involves moving somewhere where the cost of living is lower, so you can live the same lifestyle while effectively spending less. If you have a job or run a business that allows for remote working, you could consider relocating to a country with easily obtainable visas and very low costs. Classic examples of this include Thailand and Malaysia, both of which have thriving expat communities taking advantage of exactly this situation. Or, on a less dramatic scale, you could consider the fact that there are some US states that have no income tax, such as Nevada, Washington, and Alaska. Relocating to one of these states would allow you to save money that would otherwise go into the state's coffers. Of course, the trade-off here is the necessity to relocate, and this may or may not be an option—as always, it's up to you to decide what works best for you.

Then there are all the little opportunities specific to your circumstance that you can take advantage of. Many employers have schemes where they will match contributions an employee makes to their retirement fund to a certain degree. If your employer does this, you'll want to make sure to make use of it. There are also corporations that offer educational benefits, reimbursing employees for continued education while working, and most employees don't take advantage of this. If you work in the public sector, there is the Public Service Loan Forgiveness scheme, where the federal government will forgive your remaining student debt if you've been working in public service and making payments on the loan for ten years. These and many, many other opportunities are all around us, and as we saw in the hacker principle of living off the land, the hacker mindset involves being resourceful and making use of everything that is easily available.

TIME

Though money is a clear optimization point, there are a few other criteria to consider when you're setting your objectives for personal finance management. Time is an important one, of course. Perhaps the most obvious goal when it comes to managing finances is to be able to retire earlier than you'd otherwise be able to, relying on income generated from your investments.

The traditional age of retirement is sixty-five, but recent analyses have shown that the rising costs of housing and of everyday necessities are pushing that age up, and young people who are graduating from college today will be more likely to retire at the age of seventy-five. That's a long time to wait and it will leave you with a smaller proportion of your life to enjoy your retirement. Let's recall the hacker principle of being on offense. Simply accepting the status quo would mean waiting until the age of seventy-five until you're able to retire; being on offense would mean looking for alternative options and pursuing the one that's best for you, which may well be working out how to retire early. After all, no one on their deathbeds ever regretted not being able to work more—it's always the other things in life that people regret not doing, and early retirement affords you the opportunities to do them.

Straightforward early retirement is certainly a valid and viable goal, but it's also a good idea to think about what some alternative versions of retirement might look like. One option might be a period of semi-retirement, where you spend some time working only part-time before fully retiring from work. This will free up more of your time earlier on, but it will also mean that the point at which you can fully retire will be later than it would otherwise be. Another possibility to consider is that of mini-retirements, a concept popularized by Tim Ferriss. This is where you take a break from work for a short period—let's say a year or so—before returning to work, and then perhaps having subsequent other mini-retirements later on. Again, with this approach it will be longer before you can fully retire, but the advantage is that you'll have periods earlier on in your life when you can do what you want. You'll be freer to enjoy yourself during your younger years, having the opportunity to pursue things that you mightn't be able (or want) to do when you're older.

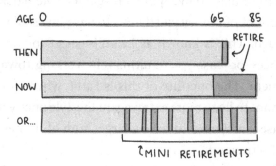

This last point leads me to the concept of time buckets. The idea is that there are periods in your life when certain experiences will be more available and more meaningful for you. If you've always wanted to spend some time skiing, it's no use waiting till you're seventy and no longer fit enough to do it, for example. Or if you want to take a year to travel around the world, that kind of endeavor is more suited to people who are in their twenties, thirties, and forties. As time passes there are certain experiences that become unachievable simply because you've aged out of them. Planning out your personal finances will help you to make sure you don't miss out on any of those experiences. Do you want to take a couple of years off work when you're thirty to go on a grand tour of the world? Then you'll want to plan your investment strategy early on to make sure you've got the money available when you hit thirty to do that.

LIFESTYLE

You will also want to think about the kind of lifestyle you want to lead once you're ready to retire, and how this will affect your investment strategy. This is an idea that has been particularly explored by members of the FIRE community (Financial Independence, Retire Early), who have shown how knowing what kind of lifestyle you want is key to working out your financial independence strategy. So, if you intend to be able to live quite a frugal lifestyle when you retire, then the amount of money you'll need to have invested will not need to be as much. This is known as LeanFl—short for Lean Financial Independence—because you're ultimately working toward having a lean retirement. The opposite of this is FatFI, where you determine that you'll want to live a more extravagant lifestyle once you've retired, in which case you'll need to have a larger sum of money invested at the point of retirement.

Both of these strategies underline the importance of knowing the type of lifestyle you'll want to be leading, but they don't really capture the true power of smart money management. For this we have to look at CoastFl. This is where you work out the age at which you want to retire and the amount of money you'll need to have invested at that point to live the lifestyle you want. Then, you invest precisely the amount you need so that you'll have accrued the necessary amount of money by the time you're ready to retire. I will go through the precise math that underlies all of this later on in this chapter, but for now I just want you to grasp the power of this approach—it means you can put aside a smaller amount of money early on in your life and then forget about it until you're ready to retire. In the meantime, you can spend the money you earn just as you'd like, without having to worry about setting any of it aside for your retirement, as that will already have been taken care of. This might mean living a more lavish lifestyle, or it might mean taking things a little easier and earning less money. In all of these cases, of course, it's important to know precisely when and how you want to be able to retire.

HAPPINESS

Finally, we have to recognize that your own happiness is an important factor in determining your objectives. After all, it's called *personal* finance for a reason—it's personal to you. You can do all the math in the world and calculate what makes the most sense on paper, but your own preferences are going to be an important factor in how you proceed.

For example, I don't drive very much. From a car insurance perspective, I qualify for the "low mileage" tier, and during the COVID-19 pandemic I drove even less. From a logical perspective it might have made sense to not have a car and just rely on taxis or public transport for whenever I have to go out. It would probably save me more money overall. But the fact is, I like owning my car and I like driving whenever I do, even if that's relatively seldom. It might not be a mathematically rational decision, but owning and driving my car makes me happy, so it's something I'm going to include in my finance strategy.

This can also apply to the concept of reclaiming time. I'm sure we've all heard the phrase "time is money," and on the face of it, this isn't an incorrect statement. Making money often does require some time investment, and so hiring someone to perform menial tasks, such as cleaning your home, may be a net benefit, since you'd be able to spend the time you would have spent on cleaning making more money than you spend on hiring a housekeeper. But there is a deeper significance at play here—time is not only money; time is also *value*.

You don't need to spend that saved time making up for the money you've spent, because simply having that time available to you is valuable. It improves the quality of your life. As such, spending money on having people perform tasks that you could have done yourself makes absolute sense, since the value is in reclaiming the time you'd have otherwise spent doing something you didn't want to do.

Another example would be how we relate to mortgages. For the vast majority of us, a house is going to be the most expensive thing we're ever going to buy, and we're going to need to take out long-term mortgages in order to do so. It can be intimidating, but it can also be an opportunity. If, for example, a mortgage comes with a 3 percent interest rate and you can reliably make a 7 percent return on money you invest, it makes sense *not* to pay off the capital on the mortgage and instead invest that money. Overall, you'll be making a 4 percent return after you deduct interest payments. Even by the time the mortgage term ends, you can easily refinance to continue the process. This is what finance experts call "leverage," and it makes sound mathematical sense. However, you may not feel comfortable knowing that you've got that debt hanging over you. Perhaps paying off that mortgage and owning the house outright with no liabilities will make you feel more secure and give you better peace of mind. If that's what you'd prefer, then that's what you need to do. As ever, your objectives are specific to your own particular circumstances. It's only after you've determined precisely what your objectives are that you can move on to the next steps of the hacker methodology.

MAKE THE MARKET WORK FOR YOU

Conducting the reconnaissance and analysis with regard to personal finances brings us to some pretty clear conclusions. As I alluded to a little earlier in this chapter, trying to make big profits by directly trading stocks on the stock exchange can be a chancy affair at best. It's by no means a reliable path to financial success. Yes, there have been successful stock traders, but if you ask someone who's just made big gains trading stocks how they did it, they're most likely going to say that they're very talented at predicting how the market is going to go. On the other hand, if you ask someone who's just made a big loss by day-trading what went wrong, they're probably going to tell you that they were just unlucky. The fact is that luck plays far too large a part in the success or failure of trading stocks to make it a reliable strategy for personal finances.

In any system, the way to make up for luck is iteration. Flip a coin once and you've got no more than an even chance of predicting whether it will come up as heads or tails. But flip the coin one thousand times and you can be pretty confident that it will come up heads around five hundred times. When it comes to investments, this kind of iteration takes the form of diversification—rather than placing all your eggs in one basket by investing in one particular stock, you can invest in a range of stocks to have a more reliable result. Index funds do exactly that—they are investment funds that are linked to stock market indexes, such as the Dow Jones or the S&P 500, automatically investing stocks across the companies listed in those indexes.

Index funds are all about diversification. You might have heard investment enthusiasts repeat the mantra "Diversify, diversify!" That's actually really good investment advice, because having a diverse investment portfolio means you're not putting all your eggs in one basket, and if one stock goes down, another might go up. I just mentioned a couple of indexes that track stocks in a selection of the biggest companies in the market, but there are other indexes that track the entire US stock market, and some that track stock markets around the world. Taking advantage of such diverse investment portfolios means you can generate a reliable return year on year. Since index funds are linked to the market, they can go up and down as the economy varies, but in the long term the US stock market index makes an average return of 10 percent per year, correcting for an average inflation rate of 3 percent, thus giving you a real-terms profit of around 7 percent a year. This makes them the perfect vehicle for managing your finances.

We started this chapter by looking at Warren Buffett as an example of a successful investor. In 2017, he expressed his support for index funds, saying: "When trillions of dollars are managed by Wall Streeters charging high fees, it will usually be the managers who reap outsized profits, not the clients. Both large and small investors should stick with low-cost index funds." He makes a very pertinent point. Stockbrokers and investment managers who actively trade stocks on behalf of their clients usually make money off of fees regardless of whether their stock trading has been successful or not. That's not to say they're not incentivized to make a profit, because they are—they make more money the more profit they make for their clients—but they do end up making money either way. In such a situation it's their clients who assume all the risk. With an index fund, however, the risks are minimal, and since most index funds are not actively managed, the fees are minimal too.

THE POWER OF COMPOUND INTEREST

Now, a 7 percent return on an investment may not seem like a very large amount. If you put in $1,000, for example, you'll make a return of $70 after one year. I know, it's not much to write home about. But the next year you'll have $1,070 invested, and the return on that will be $74.90. It's still not much more, but it *is* more. And the following year your return will increase again ($80.14 in this case), and every year not only will your profit increase, but the amount at which it increases will also increase. This is the compounding effect—the math is essentially the same as that for exponential growth. Nowadays when we say something is increasing exponentially, we often just mean that it's growing very quickly, but the reality is a little more complicated. Exponential growth usually starts off pretty slow, but as it increases the rate at which it increases also increases, so when it gets going it really does get going, and it's the same with compound interest.

All this goes to underline one crucial point: time in the market is key. Smart management of finances is all about making sure that your wealth is going to reliably grow in the long term. Warren Buffett is one of the most successful financial investors out there, but he became a billionaire only in his fifties. In fact, if you look at a graph charting his net worth over time, it looks almost exactly like an exponential growth graph, increasing slowly to begin with, then very rapidly later on.

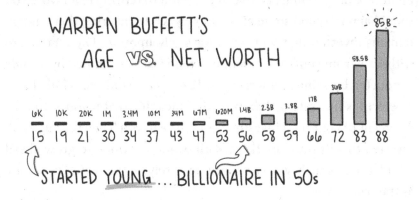

The precise math to calculate compound interest is a pretty straightforward equation, but it can be a bit fiddly to work out. A nice shortcut for that is the rule of 72—this states that dividing 72 by the interest rate will give the rough amount of time it will take for your investment to double. So, if the return on your investments is 7 percent a year, 72/7 is just over 10, giving you a figure of roughly ten years for your investment to double. After ten years your $1,000 investment will be worth $2,000, and after fifty years it'll be worth around $32,000. Of course, the more you put in to begin with, the more you'll have once it grows, and there's also nothing stopping you from adding to your investments down the line should you wish.

HOW TO SUBSIST ON YOUR WEALTH

So, the power of compound interest can help you grow your wealth, but the point of having money is not just to have it. Eventually you'll want to spend it, and ultimately the goal is to be able to leave work behind in one way or another and rely on your finances to live. But once you've spent the money, it's no longer there for you to rely upon. The answer must be that at the point of retiring from work you should aim to spend some of the money while ensuring that enough remains invested that you can always rely upon it. The amount to withdraw from your investment portfolio was determined by a study conducted by Trinity University in Texas. This study concluded that 4 percent is the "safe withdrawal rate," meaning that if you withdraw 4 percent of your total investments each year, you'll have enough still invested to withstand market volatility and continue to grow ahead of inflation. As such, you can continue to rely on that withdrawal rate as the years go by.

The corollary to this conclusion of a safe withdrawal rate of 4 percent is the rule of 25. This rule simply states that, however much money you want to be receiving in your retirement, you just multiply that figure by 25 and that'll give you the amount of money you need to invest to maintain that income. This is where the ideas of LeanFI and FatFI come in, since determining how much money you'll need to afford whatever kind of lifestyle you want to maintain will allow you to calculate how much money you'll need to have saved up in order to make that happen.

RULE OF 25

4% RULE

IN YOUR RETIREMENT

YOU'LL NEED THIS MUCH MONEY INVESTED:	IF YOU WANT THIS MUCH MONEY		
	PER DAY:	PER MONTH:	PER YEAR:
$2,500,000	$274	$8,333	$100,000
$2,250,000	$247	$7,500	$90,000
$2,000,000	$219	$6,667	$80,000
$1,750,000	$192	$5,833	$70,000
$1,500,000	$164	$5,000	$60,000
$1,250,000	$137	$4,167	$50,000
$1,000,000	$110	$3,333	$40,000
$750,000	$82	$2,500	$30,000
$500,000	$55	$1,667	$20,000
$250,000	$27	$833	$10,000

Put that together with the rule of 72 for compound interest and you have all the math laid out to work out what you need to do in order to retire. First you need to work out what kind of an annual income you'll need in retirement. Will you be cutting back on your spending, or will you want to lead a more opulent lifestyle? How much is that going to cost? Multiply that by 25 and you have the amount of money you'll need at the point of retiring. Then determine when you want to retire and you know how long you have to build up that amount of money. Using the rule of 72 (or the actual compound interest equation or an online calculator if you want to be more precise), you can work out how much money you'll need to have invested in order to reach that figure at the correct time.

For example, let's say you want to have an income of $30,000 a year in retirement and you want to retire in thirty years. $30,000 multiplied by 25 is $750,000, so you have thirty years to get to that figure. Using the rule of 72, you know that investing in index funds returning around 7 percent a year will mean you'll roughly double your money every ten years—there are three lots of ten in thirty, so dividing $750,000 by two three times is $93,750. That's how much you need to invest today in order to reach your goal of $750,000 in thirty years from today. If you have that money available and can do that straightaway, then fantastic—that's what we call CoastFI. You've done all the math, invested the correct amount of money, and are all set for retirement. If you don't have the money to invest yet, then that's something you can work toward. As I mentioned earlier, you need money to make money, and some of the suggestions I've made should come in handy in generating the money needed to invest.

Finally, do you remember when I talked about Mr. Money Mustache way back in chapter five? He was the one who worked out how much money he'd need to save from his income in order to retire after a certain number of years. As it so happens, a lot of this math was behind his calculations. What he added into the mix, however, was continued investment. He didn't just look at investing a certain amount of money at one point then leaving the rest all to compound interest, but he considered continuously saving and investing a certain proportion of his income, which in addition to the compounding effect would allow his retirement to grow even more quickly. It was this that led him to conclude that saving 50 percent of one's income and investing that in reliable index funds would allow one to retire after only seventeen years (see table on page 201).

This is particularly pertinent to the execute stage of the hacker methodology. Depending on the conclusions you draw from your objectives, reconnaissance, and analysis, it may be the case that the execution will involve simply dumping a substantial amount of capital in an index fund and waiting, particularly if you've decided to take the CoastFI route. But if you've decided to take a more active plan for your finances, you'll need to stick to it for long enough to allow the math to work out. This is a good time to remember the hacker characteristic of courage—if you, like Mr. Money Mustache, decide to invest 50 percent of your income, you're going to have to live with the fact that for a while you'll have half the money you're earning at your disposal, and you'll need to persist with that strategy until it pays its dividends.

SAVINGS RATE (%)	WORKING YEARS UNTIL RETIREMENT
5	66
10	51
15	43
20	37
25	32
30	28
35	25
40	22
45	19
50	17
55	14.5
60	12.5
65	10.5
70	8.5
75	7
80	5.5
85	4
90	< 3
95	< 2
100	ZERO

REASSESS

As usual, we mustn't overlook the reassess stage of the hacker methodology. Yes, you've worked your objectives, and you know when you want to retire and what kind of an income you'll want to have then. You've done all the math, worked out how much money you'll need to invest and when, and you've put your investment plan into action. You can just sit back and let everything work itself out, and it may very well be that you'll never make any adjustments and rely on that plan, but you should also always be tuned in to the fact that your objectives might change.

Take this as an example: The rule of 25 and the 4 percent safe withdrawal rate are based on the idea of maintaining your invested capital ahead of inflation in perpetuity. Now, I don't want to be too morbid, but the fact is that none of us is going to live forever and, as they say, wealth is all very well but you can't take it with you. As such, maintaining that capital forever may not make sense, so you might want to look at withdrawing at a higher rate in retirement, meaning that it will deplete eventually, but you'll be making more of it while you're still around. Of course, it might be that you have children and you want to make sure that when you die that wealth will be there for them to inherit. Or it might be the case that when you worked out your objectives and your finance plans you were planning on having kids one day, but later down the line you decide you're definitely not going to have kids. Or conversely, you might have never seen yourself becoming a parent but then some years later you end up having children. Or it could be something completely different—it could be you originally planned for a leaner retirement but later decided you'd prefer a slightly more lavish lifestyle.

Any of these decisions will change your objectives, and your investment strategy should change accordingly. You should take a step back and review things every so often, perhaps every five years or at major milestones in your life like getting married, or emigrating, or anything else. Are your finance objectives still aligned with what you want? If not, how should they be adjusted? Once you've answered those questions, it's a simple case of reviewing the math and seeing what adjustments are needed to ensure that, no matter what happens, your path to financial freedom is secure.

Finale

HACKING THE SYSTEMS AND BEYOND

Well, we've gone through quite a journey together over the course of this book.

We've seen how hackers take advantage of systems to achieve the outcomes they want and we've recognized how we can apply this approach to all aspects of our lives. We looked at the difference between the hacker mindset and the slacker mindset and saw how the slacker mindset is not just about a lack of execution but can also be manifested as a lack of planning. Crucially, we came to the image of the pendulum, an image that we've frequently gone back to in later chapters, which shows that embodying the hacker mindset means constantly swinging back and forth between planning and execution in perfect equilibrium, never getting too hung up on one side or the other.

We went on to explore some of the characteristics a hacker will have. We saw that a hacker will demonstrate the **curiosity** to try out new things; will be driven to seek **constant improvement** in what they do; will have the **courage** to take risks; will exhibit the **determination** to keep on going in the face of adversity; will take a **realistic** approach in recognizing what can and cannot be achieved; and will strive to be **efficient** to ensure that the maximum gain can be achieved from the minimum amount of effort or cost. We also saw how the various characteristics can be combined and used together to create super-characteristics.

This took us on to the hacker principles. With Hacker Principle 1 we talked about how it's important to always **be on offense**, driving the change you want to see to achieve your goals, while also recognizing that being *on* offense doesn't mean *being* offensive. In Hacker Principle 2 we explored the idea of **reverse engineering** and saw how analyzing the systems that are already out there, and pushing at their limits, provides an advantage in overcoming those systems. The third principle brought us to the concept of **living off the land**, which showed us that there are easily accessible resources all around us, and making use of them is a key part of achieving your goals with the hacker mindset. Hacker Principle 4 considered the topic of determining **risk**, where I talked about how to calculate expected value and weigh the balance between cost and gain when it comes to considering various approaches. In Hacker Principle 5 we looked at the concept of **social engineering** and how taking advantage of human interactions and expectations is often a key part of making a system work for you. With the sixth and final principle we emphasized the importance of **pivoting**, being able to change your plan as required when confronted with unexpected events as well as making sure to make use of any points of leverage attained during the process, even those you did not expect.

We then came to what might be considered the crux of this book: the hacker methodology. This is the process that lays out how to apply all these characteristics and principles in a systematic way. You will first establish your **objectives**, determining precisely what it is you want to achieve, whether that be on a microscopic or macroscopic level. You will then conduct **reconnaissance**, gathering information and learning everything you need about the relevant systems at play. Next you will do your **analysis**, processing the information you've gathered and working out precisely what your plan of action will be. With the following step you will **execute** and put your plan into action, ensuring that you don't get hung up on the planning side of the pendulum. The final and most important step of the hacker methodology is to **reassess**—this is where you consider how well your plan is working, whether it needs any adjustments, and whether your objectives might have changed. You might also consider whether or not you can simply call your project a success and move on to the next one. The final step of the methodology brings you back to the first, and it's the cyclical nature of the hacker methodology that allows you to ensure that you always remain on top.

Having established the methodology, we looked at a few particular examples of how it can work in your life. We thought about how the hacker mindset can be applied to your career in employed work, whether that's how to increase your income, how to succeed when it comes to promotions and pay raises, or how to get a job in the first place. We also looked at applying the hacker mindset in the context of business, both in working out the best kind of business for you and in maximizing your chances of success. We finally looked at personal finances and how the hacker mindset can help you to retire when you want, giving you the financial freedom to live the life you desire.

Of course, these are only a few examples of how the hacker mindset can work in practice—the number of other possible applications is practically limitless. Education is a system that can be hacked, so if you want to improve your grades or simply learn more for the sake of it, the hacker mindset is there for you. Or perhaps you just want to have better productivity in your life in general; apply the hacker mindset and you can make it happen. Even dating is a system, so if you want to improve things in your love life, you just need to approach it with the hacker mindset. And that's just the tip of the tip of the iceberg; there's no telling how many more possibilities there are.

WE NEED HACKERS NOW MORE THAN EVER

We currently live in a world where there are far too many people who are simply cogs in a great machine. People who don't ask questions and just accept things as they are, who just get on with their lives because, though it's not perfect, it's "good enough." People who sense that they're not achieving what they want to achieve, or who feel that they are trapped within their jobs, but who can't see the system for what it is and have no idea how to overcome it. More and more over the years, corporations have become bigger, savvier, and more ruthless. Large corporations know how to make use of systems and are fundamentally motivated by profits, not the welfare of the people involved. They like nothing more than to set up complex systems that are full of automatons unquestioningly fulfilling their roles to the benefit of the company, but not to themselves. And as with corporations, so with society itself—when you simply and unquestioningly play by the rules, it's the people on top who win, not you. The hacker mindset is here to change that.

We need more people to take ownership of their own destinies. We need people to stop going with the flow, simply accepting the status quo and working to the agenda of others. I certainly don't look down upon such people—as I said at the beginning of this book, I was one myself—but I genuinely believe that the world would be a better place if more people broke free of these systems to work toward their own aspirations and goals. This is really the mission of *The Hacker Mindset*.

The hacker mindset is a great equalizer. By breaking free and making the system work for us, we shall reclaim our power and progress closer toward a more balanced society.

And, of course, this book is just the beginning. I've set out the hacker mindset, I've explained the principles and the hacker methodology, but you're the one who's going to apply it and put it into action—whether that's in your job, your business aspirations, or your finances; with regard to your general productivity or your love life; or in hundreds of other circumstances I haven't even thought of. Make use of hacker-level curiosity and courage to push the boundaries of the systems around you and of the hacker mindset itself, coming up with new and inventive ways of making it work.

It's time to go out there and get hacking!

ACKNOWLEDGMENTS

I am incredibly grateful to my team, friends, and family who supported me through the book-writing process. You all are awesome. Much love and see you soon.

Hasan Kubba, Hussain Ajina, Ash Ali, Jason Bartholomew, Matt Holt, Katie Dickman, Alex Chaveriat, Matt Mullins, Todd Brison, John Pingelton, Trudi Affield, Liz Wanic, Joe Grand, yaxis, Stephen Thomas, Lee Anderson, Kurt Grutzmacher, Peter Kim, Marten Mickos.

Rusty Huber, Troy Brown, Justin Trujilo, Joshua Marpet, Mike McPherson, May McDonough, Marv White, Jacque Blanchard, E Pierce, Andrew Shumate, Jim Hofstee, Gr3y R0n1n, Sam Estrella, Renee Alderman, Kevin Sugihara, Rachel Sugihara, Jim McMurry, Dragos Ruiu, Russ Bodnyk, Jeremiah Grossman, Zach Lanier, Willo Sana, Gresham Lochner, Tynan, Pamela Narowski, Andrew Hutton, Rahul Brahmbhatt, Alma Lugtu, Jordan Grumet, Gwen Merz, Amberly Grant, Travis Marziani, Andrew Youderian, Ali Abdaal, Ian Schoen, Andrew Barry, Marie Poulin, Robbie Crabtree.

Stephen Cospolich, Devin Ertel, Allison Wikoff, Miles Tracy, Seth Bromberger, Jimmy Dang, Charles Tsai, Kevin Luke, Adrian Holguin, Jia Ye, Nick Baronian, Pieralberto Deganello, Nick Stanescu, Joe Leonard, Jeremy Brotherton, Gerry Collins, Matt Schlereth, Joonho Lee, Jeremy Schley, Anthony Grandle, Kevin Bang, Dave Kennedy, Shannon Morse, Jason Blanchard, Darren Kitchen.

RECOMMENDED BOOKS

Principle 1: Be on Offense

Allende, Sam Connif. *Be More Pirate, or How to Take on the World and Win.* New York: Touchstone, 2018.

Lafley, A. G. *Playing to Win: How Strategy Really Works.* Boston: Harvard Business Review Press, 2013.

Principle 2: Reverse Engineering

Bet-David, Patrick. *Your Next Five Moves: Master the Art of Business Strategy.* New York: Gallery Books, 2020.

Friedman, Ron. *Decoding Greatness: How the Best in the World Reverse Engineer Success.* New York: Simon & Schuster, 2021.

Principle 3: Living Off the Land

Ferriss, Tim. *The 4-Hour Chef: The Simple Path to Cooking Like a Pro, Learning Anything, and Living the Good Life.* Boston: New Harvest, 2012.

Kaufman, Josh. *The First 20 Hours: How to Learn Anything—Fast.* New York: Portfolio/Penguin, 2013.

Kleon, Austin. *Steal Like an Artist: 10 Things Nobody Told You About Being Creative.* New York: Workman, 2012.

♟ Sullivan, Dan. *Who Not How: The Formula to Achieve Bigger Goals Through Accelerating Teamwork*. Carlsbad, CA: Hay House, 2020.

Principle 4: Risk

♟ Duhigg, Charles. *Smarter Faster Better: The Secrets of Being Productive in Life and Business*. New York: Random House, 2016.

♟ Duke, Annie. *How to Decide: Simple Tools for Making Better Choices*. New York: Portfolio, 2020.

♟ Duke, Annie. *Thinking in Bets: Making Smarter Decisions When You Don't Have All the Facts*. New York: Portfolio/ Penguin, 2018.

♟ Koch, Richard. *The 80/20 Principle: The Secret to Achieving More with Less*. New York: Doubleday, 1999.

Principle 5: Social Engineering

♟ Carnegie, Dale. *How to Win Friends and Influence People*. New York: Simon & Schuster, 1936.

♟ Hadnagy, Christopher. *Human Hacking: Win Friends, Influence People, and Leave Them Better Off for Having Met You*. New York: Harper Business, 2021.

♟ Voss, Chris. *Never Split the Difference: Negotiating As If Your Life Depended On It*. New York: Harper Business, 2016.

Principle 6: Pivot

♟ de Bono, Edward. *Lateral Thinking: Creativity Step by Step*. London: Penguin UK, 2010.

♟ Syed, Matthew. *Black Box Thinking: Why Most People Never Learn from Their Mistakes—But Some Do*. New York: Portfolio/Penguin, 2015.

🛐   Wiseman, Liz with Greg McKeown. *Multipliers: How the Best Leaders Make Everyone Smarter*. New York: Harper Business, 2010.

Mindset

🛐   Altucher, James. *Skip the Line: The 10,000 Experiments Rule and Other Surprising Advice for Reaching Your Goals*. New York: Harper Business, 2021.

🛐   Dalio, Ray. *Principles: Life & Work*. New York: Simon & Schuster, 2017.

🛐   Dweck, Carol. *Mindset: The New Psychology of Success*. New York: Random House, 2006.

🛐   Forleo, Marie. *Everything Is Figureoutable*. New York: Portfolio/Penguin, 2019.

🛐   Galef, Julia. *The Scout Mindset: Why Some People See Things Clearly and Others Don't*. New York: Portfolio, 2021.

🛐   Godin, Seth. *Linchpin: Are You Indispensable?* New York: Portfolio, 2010.

🛐   Schwartz, David Joseph. *The Magic of Thinking Big*. New York: Touchstone, 2015.

🛐   Snow, Shane. *Smartcuts: How Hackers, Innovators, and Icons Accelerate Success*. New York: Harper Business, 2014.

🛐   Vaynerchuk, Gary. *Twelve and a Half: Leveraging the Emotional Ingredients Necessary for Business Success*. New York: Harper Business, 2021.

Finance

🛐   Housel, Morgan. *The Psychology of Money: Timeless Lessons on Wealth, Greed, and Happiness*. Hampshire, UK: Harriman House, 2020.

🛐   Perkins, Bill. *Die with Zero: Getting All You Can from Your Money and Your Life*. Boston: Houghton Mifflin Harcourt, 2020.

🔑 Robin, Vicki. *Your Money or Your Life: 9 Steps to Transforming Your Relationship with Money and Achieving Financial Independence*. New York: Penguin Books, 2008.

🔑 Sabatier, Grant. *Financial Freedom: A Proven Path to All the Money You Will Ever Need*. New York: Avery, 2019.

SELECTED
BIBLIOGRAPHY

Introduction
Eyal, Nir. *Hooked: How to Build Habit-Forming Products.* New York: Portfolio, 2014.

Chapter 2: The Two Mindsets: Hacker Versus Slacker
"Genius Is One Percent Inspiration, Ninety-Nine Percent Perspiration." Quote Investigator, December 14, 2012. https://quoteinvestigator.com/2012/12/14/genius-ratio/.

Ziegler, Maseena. "7 Famous Quotes You Definitely Didn't Know Were From Women." *Forbes*, September 1, 2014. https://www.forbes.com/sites/maseenaziegler/2014/09/01/how-we-all-got-it-wrong-women-were-behind-these-7-famously-inspiring-quotes/.

Chapter 3: The Characteristics of a Hacker
Bunkley, Nick. "Joseph Juran, 103, Pioneer in Quality Control, Dies." *New York Times*, March 3, 2008. https://www.nytimes.com/2008/03/03/business/03juran.html.

Clear, James. *Atomic Habits: An Easy & Proven Way to Build Good Habits & Break Bad Ones*. New York: Avery, 2018.

"CWE Top 25 Most Dangerous Software Errors." SANS. https://www.sans.org/top25-software-errors/.

"Every Child Is an Artist. The Problem Is How to Remain an Artist Once He or She Grows Up." Quote Investigator, March 7, 2015. https://quoteinvestigator.com/2015/03/07/child-art/.

Hayes, Adam. "The Peter Principle: What It Is and How to Overcome It." Investopedia, August 30, 2023. https://www.investopedia.com/terms/p/peter-principle.asp.

"OWASP Top Ten." OWASP. https://owasp.org/www-project-top-ten/.

"The Offsec OSCP song Try Harder." Muh. Andry Amiruddin, February 4, 2018. YouTube video, 3:24. https://youtu.be/t-bgRQfeW64.

Savage, Adam. "Mike Rowe and MythBusters' Educational Impact." Adam Savage's Tested, December 11, 2022. YouTube video, 11:19. https://youtu.be/BNu2QDiMBHA.

Stack Overflow 2022 Developer Survey. https://survey.stackoverflow.co/2022/.

Yaneer Bar-Yam. "Concepts: Power Law." New England Complex Systems Institute, 2011. http://www.necsi.edu/guide/concepts/powerlaw.html.

Chapter 4: Hacker Principle 1: Be on Offense

Chase, Chris. "Is This the End for Roger Federer?" *FOX Sports,* July 27, 2016. Archived from the original, https://web.archive.org/web/20190421214011/https://www.foxsports.com/tennis/story/is-this-the-end-for-roger-federer-072716.

Eccleshare, Charlie. "Why Roger Federer Will Never Win Another Grand Slam." *Daily Telegraph*, May 3, 2016. Archived from the original, https://ghostarchive.org/archive/VZ6Yp.

Frick, Walter. "How to Survive a Recession and Thrive Afterward." *Harvard Business Review*, 2019. https://hbr.org/2019/05/how-to -survive-a-recession-and-thrive-afterward.

Greenberg, Andy. "The Confessions of Marcus Hutchins, the Hacker Who Saved the Internet." Wired, May 12, 2020. Archived from the original, https://web.archive.org/web/20200512121004 /https://www.wired.com/story/confessions-marcus-hutchins -hacker-who-saved-the-internet/.

Gulati, Ranjay, Nitin Nohria, and Franz Wohlgezogen. "Roaring Out of Recession." *Harvard Business Review*, March 2010. https://hbr .org/2010/03/roaring-out-of-recession.

Knopper, Steve. "iTunes' 10th Anniversary: How Steve Jobs Turned the Industry Upside Down." *Rolling Stone*, April 26, 2013. https:// www.rollingstone.com/culture/culture-news/itunes-10th -anniversary-how-steve-jobs-turned-the-industry-upside-down -68985/.

O'Shannessy, Craig. "Think You Missed Roger Federer At His Peak? Think Again | ATP Tour | Tennis." *ATP Tour*, December 28, 2017. Archived from the original, https://web.archive.org/web /20200607170223/https://www.atptour.com/en/news/federer -serving-his-best-infosys-2017.

Pingue, Frank. ""Federer's Comeback Season 'Off the Charts', Says Pundits." *Reuters*, August 24, 2017. Archived from the original, https://web.archive.org/web/20200607170215/https://www .reuters.com/article/us-tennis-usopen-federer-idUSKCN1B42E7.

"SCADA Systems and the Terrorist Threat: Protecting the Nation's Critical Control Systems." Joint Hearing, House of Representatives, One Hundred Ninth Congress, First Session, October 18, 2005: 18–23. www.fas.org/irp/congress/2005_hr /scada.pdf.

Chapter 5: Hacker Principle 2: Reverse Engineering

"APT3." Attack.Mitre.org. https://attack.mitre.org/groups/G0022/.

"APT3: A Nation-State Sponsored Adversary Responsible for Multiple High Profile Campaigns." Cyware. https://cyware.com/blog/apt3 -a-nation-state-sponsored-adversary-responsible-for-multiple -high-profile-campaigns-f58c.

Basu, Tanya. "Spilling Silicon Valley's Secrets, One Tweet at a Time." *MIT Technology Review*, April 22, 2022. https://www.technology review.com/2022/04/22/1049460/silicon-valley-secrets-twitter -jane-manchun-wong/.

"The Birth of a Company." Dell. https://www.dell.com/learn/aw/en /awcorp1/birth-of-company.

Dell, Michael, and Catherine Fredman. *Direct from Dell: Strategies That Revolutionized an Industry*. New York: Harper Business, 1999.

Dussault, Mike. "Notebook: Belichick Talks Film Study Evolution." Patriots.com, January 7, 2022. https://www.patriots.com/news /notebook-belichick-talks-film-study-evolution.

Horwitz, Darrell. "Moneyball: The Truth About Billy Beane and His Role with the Oakland Athletics." Bleacher Report, September 22, 2011. https://bleacherreport.com/articles/857869-moneyball -the-truth-about-billy-beane-and-his-role-with-the-oakland -athletics.

Konig, Joe. "Play It Faster, Play It Weirder: How Speedrunning Pushes Video Games Beyond Their Limits." *The Guardian*, September 28, 2021. https://www.theguardian.com/culture/2021/sep/29/play-it -faster-play-it-weirder-how-speedrunning-pushes-video-games -beyond-their-limits.

Lewis, Michael D. *Moneyball: The Art of Winning an Unfair Game*. New York: W. W. Norton, 2003.

Sirk, Christopher. "Xerox PARC and the Origins of GUI." CRM.org, June 12, 2020. https://crm.org/articles/xerox-parc-and-the-origins -of-gui.

Szczepaniak, John. "Feature: The Story of the Game Genie, the Cheat Device Nintendo Tried (And Failed) to Kill." *Nintendo Life*, December 26, 2021. https://www.nintendolife.com/features

/the-story-of-the-game-genie-the-cheat-device-nintendo-tried
-and-failed-to-kill.

Chapter 6: Hacker Principle 3: Living Off the Land

"A Breakdown and Analysis of the December, 2014 Sony Hack." Risk-
Based Security, December 5, 2014. Archived from the original,
https://web.archive.org/web/20160304042516/https://www
.riskbasedsecurity.com/2014/12/a-breakdown-and-analysis-of
-the-december-2014-sony-hack/.

cedriclGV/awesome-finance. Github.com. https://github.com
/cedriclGV/awesome-finance.

"Disaster Movie," April 25, 2021. In *The Lazarus Heist*, produced by
BBC. Podcast, 36:46. https://www.bbc.co.uk/sounds/play
/p09fktyl.

Gee, Garrett. "Free MacWorld Expo Platinum Pass." *Garrett Gee*
(blog), January 14, 2008. https://garrettgee.com/cyber-security
/free-macworld-expo-platinum-pass/.

Grutzmacher, Kurt. "Another Free MacWorld Platinum Pass? Yes in
2008!" *Superimposing Nothing Nowhere* (blog), January 14, 2008.
http://grutztopia.jingojango.net/2008/01/another-free-macworld
-platinum-pass-yes.html.

Grutzmacher, Kurt. "Your Free MacWorld Expo Platinum Pass (valued
at $1,695)." *Superimposing Nothing Nowhere* (blog), January 11,
2007. http://grutztopia.jingojango.net/2007/01/your-free
-macworld-expo-platinum-pass_11.html.

Keith, Bonnie. *Strategic Sourcing in the New Economy*. New York:
Palgrave Macmillan, 2016.

"Kill Switch," June 20, 2021. In *The Lazarus Heist*, produced by BBC.
Podcast, 45:07. https://www.bbc.co.uk/sounds/play/p09m14pt.

KrishMunot/awesome-startup. Github.com. https://github.com
/KrishMunot/awesome-startup.

"Lazarus Group." ATT&CK, May 31, 2017. Last modified March 30,
2023. https://attack.mitre.org/groups/G0032/.

Lee, Martin, Warren Mercer, Paul Rascagneres, and Craig Williams. "Player 3 Has Entered the Game: Say Hello to 'WannaCry.'" *Talos Intelligence* (blog), May 12, 2017. Archived from the original, https://web.archive.org/web/20210604030643/https://blog .talosintelligence.com/2017/05/wannacry.html.

Leonardo da Vinci Quotes. Goodreads. https://www.goodreads.com /author/quotes/13560.Leonardo_da_Vinci.

"Living Off the Land Binaries, Scripts and Libraries." LOLBAS. https://lolbas-project.github.io/.

LOLBAS-Project/LOLBAS. Github.com. https://github.com/LOLBAS -Project/LOLBAS.

McCartney, Scott. "Miles for Nothing: How the Government Helped Frequent Fliers Make a Mint." *Wall Street Journal*, December 7, 2009. https://www.wsj.com/amp/articles /SB126014168569179245.

Menn, Joseph, and Indraneel Sur. "Microsoft Goof Makes a $400 Shoppers' Gift." *Los Angeles Times*, January 7, 2000. https://www .latimes.com/archives/la-xpm-2000-jan-07-mn-51627-story.html.

Secrets of the Dead. Season 16, episode 4, "Leonardo, the Man Who Saved Science." Aired April 5, 2017, on PBS. https://www.pbs.org /wnet/secrets/leonardo-man-saved-science-preview/3462/.

sindresorhus/awesome. Github.com. https://github.com/ sindresorhus/awesome.

"35 Inspirational Michelangelo Quotes (SCULPTOR)." Graciousquotes.com, March 8, 2023. https://graciousquotes.com /michelangelo/.

Chapter 7: Hacker Principle 4: Risk

Bruner, Raisa. "A Complete Timeline of Elon Musk's Business Endeavors." *Time*, April 27, 2022. https://time.com/6170834 /elon-musk-business-timeline-twitter/.

Chen, James. "Alpha: What It Means in Investing, with Examples." Investopedia, May 25, 2023. https://www.investopedia.com /terms/a/alpha.asp.

Kagan, Noah (@noahkagan). "You should ALWAYS ask for a discount." Twitter, May 20, 2020, 2:54 p.m. https://twitter.com /noahkagan/status/1263181206314561536?lang=en.

"The Lottery: Is It Ever Worth Playing?" Investopedia, October 9, 2023. https://www.investopedia.com/managing-wealth/worth -playing-lottery/.

Oliver, John. "Televangelists: *Last Week Tonight with John Oliver* (HBO)." LastWeekTonight, August 17, 2015. YouTube video, 20:05. https://youtu.be/7y1xJAVZxXg?si=FPyPv_Br9iYFk8hk.

Perlroth, Nicole. "Security Experts Expect 'Shellshock' Software Bug in Bash to Be Significant." *New York Times*, September 25, 2014. https://www.nytimes.com/2014/09/26/technology/security -experts-expect-shellshock-software-bug-to-be-significant.html.

Shontell, Alyson. "Why Everyone Should Purposely Sit in the Wrong Seat on an Airplane at Least Once." *Business Insider*, August 10, 2014. https://www.businessinsider.com/noah-kagans-coffee -challenge-helps-you-get-over-fear-2014-8.

Chapter 8: Hacker Principle 5: Social Engineering

"Doppelganger Domains." Godai Group. https://godaigroup.net /publications/doppelganger-domains/.

"Getting Started: The Four Tendencies." Gretchen Rubin. https:// gretchenrubin.com/four-tendencies/.

Kinne, Troy, and Steve Philp. "CAN YOU GET IN ANYWHERE WITH A LADDER?" Troy Kinne, June 8, 2015. YouTube video, 3:18. https://youtu.be/NiEMcjSQOzg?si=PA0LMEdRTotY4iJu.

"Myers-Briggs® Overview." Myers & Briggs Foundation. https:// www.myersbriggs.org/my-mbti-personality-type/mbti-basics/.

"The Nine Enneagram Type Descriptions." The Enneagram
    Institute. 2023. https://www.enneagraminstitute.com/type
    -descriptions.

O'Sullivan, Donie, Brian Fung, and Evan Perez. "Twitter Says Some
    Accounts Had Personal Data Stolen in Massive Hack." CNN
    Business, July 18, 2020. https://edition.cnn.com/2020/07/18
    /tech/twitter-hack-data-downloaded/index.html.

"Sockpuppet." CyberWire. https://thecyberwire.com/glossary
    /sockpuppet.

Toulas, Bill. "Hackers Now Use 'Sock Puppets' for More Realistic
    Phishing Attacks." BleepingComputer, September 13, 2022.
    https://www.bleepingcomputer.com/news/security/hackers-now
    -use-sock-puppets-for-more-realistic-phishing-attacks/.

Zetter, Kim. "Researchers' Typosquatting Stole 20 GB of E-Mail from
    Fortune 500." *Wired*, September 8, 2011. https://www.wired.com
    /2011/09/doppelganger-domains/.

Chapter 9: Hacker Principle 6: Pivot

Ali Abdaal website home page. https://aliabdaal.com/.

Ali Abdaal YouTube channel. https://www.youtube.com/c/aliabdaal.

Chris Sacca website home page. https://chrissacca.com/.

Drozhzhin, Alex. "Black Hat USA 2015: The Full Story of How That
    Jeep Was Hacked." Kaspersky, August 7, 2015. https://usa
    .kaspersky.com/blog/blackhat-jeep-cherokee-hack-explained
    /5749/.

Greenberg, Andy. "Hackers Remotely Kill a Jeep on the Highway—
    With Me in It." *Wired*, July 21, 2015. https://www.wired.com
    /2015/07/hackers-remotely-kill-jeep-highway/.

Miller, Charlie, and Chris Valasek. "Remote Exploitation of an
    Unaltered Passenger Vehicle." Black Hat, December 29, 2015.
    YouTube video, 51:34. https://youtu.be/MAcHkASmXEc?si=
    L32zA_xo88OPIa82.

Palmer, Emily. "A Fake Heiress Called Anna Delvey Conned the City's Wealthy. 'I'm Not Sorry,' She Says." *New York Times*, May 10, 2019. Archived from the original, https://web.archive.org /web/20210403130655/https://www.nytimes.com/2019/05/10 /nyregion/anna-delvey-sorokin.html.

Pressler, Jessica. "Maybe She Had So Much Money She Just Lost Track of It." *New York*, May 2018. https://www.thecut.com /article/how-anna-delvey-tricked-new-york.html.

Rouse, Margaret. "What Is Watering Hole Attack?" SearchSecurity. https://www.techtarget.com/searchsecurity/definition/watering -hole-attack.

"Supply Chain Security Guidance." National Cyber Security Centre. https://www.ncsc.gov.uk/collection/supply-chain-security /watering-hole-attacks.

Chapter 10: The Hacker Methodology

Clear, James. "Warren Buffett's '2 List' Strategy: How to Maximize Your Focus and Master Your Priorities." *James Clear* (blog). https://jamesclear.com/buffett-focus.

"The Covey Time Management Matrix Explained." Indeed, July 22, 2022. https://www.indeed.com/career-advice/career-development /covey-time-management-matrix.

"The Eisenhower Matrix: How to Prioritize Your To-Do List." Asana, October 4, 2022. https://asana.com/resources/eisenhower-matrix.

"The 4 Quadrants of Time Management Matrix [Guide]." Timeular, April 30, 2023. https://timeular.com/blog/time-management -matrix/.

"Introducing the Eisenhower Matrix." Eisenhower. https://www .eisenhower.me/eisenhower-matrix/.

Sethi, Ramit. "Here's How to Know If Your Business Idea Is Actually Good." I Will Teach You to Be Rich, December 13, 2016. https:// www.iwillteachyoutoberich.com/how-do-i-know-if-my-ideas -are-good/.

Sethi, Ramit. "I Don't Just Launch a Product and Pray. Here's What I Do." I Will Teach You to Be Rich, May 24, 2017. https://www .iwillteachyoutoberich.com/i-dont-just-launch-a-product-and -pray-heres-what-i-do/.

"Steps of the Scientific Method." Science Buddies. https://www .sciencebuddies.org/science-fair-projects/science-fair/steps-of -the-scientific-method.

"What Is Warren Buffett's 5/25 rule?" Quora. https://www.quora .com/What-is-Warren-Buffetts-5-25-rule.

Chapter 11: Corporate Career × Hacker Mindset

Greenwald, John. "Rank and Fire." *Time*, June 11, 2001. https:// content.time.com/time/business/article/0,8599,129988,00.html.

McLean, Bethany, and Peter Elkind. *The Smartest Guys in the Room: The Amazing Rise and Scandalous Fall of Enron.* New York: Portfolio, 2003: 28. https://archive.org/details/ smartestguysin00mcle/page/28/mode/2up.

Chapter 12: Entrepreneurship × Hacker Mindset

"Amazon FBA: Fulfillment Services for Your Ecommerce Business." Amazonhttps://sell.amazon.com/fulfillment-by-amazon.

Balfour, Brian. "Product Channel Fit Will Make or Break Your Growth Strategy." *BrianBalfour.com* (blog), July 12, 2017. https:// brianbalfour.com/essays/product-channel-fit-for-growth.

"Bombas Giving." Bombas. https://bombas.com/pages/giving-back.

Crockett, Zachary. "*Shark Tank* Deep Dive: A Data Analysis of All 10 seasons." *The Hustle*, May 19, 2019. https://thehustle.co/shark -tank-data-analysis-10-seasons/.

Eatough, Erin. "What Is Ikigai and How Can It Change My Life?" BetterUp, May 7, 2021. https://www.betterup.com/blog/what-is -ikigai.

Hartmans, Avery, Sarah Jackson, Azmi Haroun, and Sam Tabahriti. "The Rise and Fall of Elizabeth Holmes, the Former Theranos

CEO Whose Prison Term Has Been Shortened by 2 Years."
    Business Insider, July 11, 2023. https://www.businessinsider.com
    /theranos-founder-ceo-elizabeth-holmes-life-story-bio-2018-4.

McIntyre, Georgia. "What Percentage of Small Businesses Fail? (And
    Other Need-to-Know Stats)." Fundera, November 20, 2020.
    https://www.fundera.com/blog/what-percentage-of-small
    -businesses-fail.

O'Brien, Sara Ashley. "The Rise and Fall of Elizabeth Holmes: A
    Timeline." CNN Business, November 17, 2022. https://www
    .cnn.com/2022/01/04/tech/elizabeth-holmes-rise-and-fall/index
    .html.

Pressler, Jessica. "Maybe She Had So Much Money She Just Lost
    Track of It." *New York*, May 2018. https://www.thecut.com
    /article/how-anna-delvey-tricked-new-york.html.

Sanchez, Codie (@realcodiesanchez). TikTok profile. https://www
    .tiktok.com/@realcodiesanchez.

Chapter 13: Personal Finance × Hacker Mindset

Cooley, Philip L., Carl M. Hubband, and Daniel T. Walz. "Retirement
    Savings: Choosing a Withdrawal Rate That Is Sustainable." AAII
    Journal, February 1998. https://www.aaii.com/files/pdf/6794
    _retirement-savings-choosing-a-withdrawal-rate-that-is
    -sustainable.pdf.

Ferriss, Tim. "How to Take a Mini-Retirement: Tips and Tricks." *Tim
    Ferriss* (blog), June 4, 2008. https://tim.blog/2008/06/04/how-to
    -take-a-mini-retirement-tips-and-tricks/.

Hoffower, Hillary. "Forget Early Retirement—People Who Saved
    Enough Money to Travel for Weeks or Years Say a 'Mini-
    Retirement Is Just as Rewarding." *Business Insider*, August 2, 2019.
    https://www.businessinsider.com/early-retirement-vs-mini
    -retirement-advice-how-to-save-2018-6.

Perkins, Bill. *Die with Zero: Getting All You Can from Your Money and
    Your Life*. Boston: Mariner Books, 2020.

Perkins, Bill. "Forget the Bucket List: Use 'Time Buckets' to Plan a
    Meaningful Life." *Business Insider*, July 28, 2020. https://www
    .businessinsider.com/forget-bucket-list-use-time-buckets-to
    -plan-meaningful-life-2020-7.

Loudenback, Tanza. "There Are 3 Main Types of Early Retirement,
    and the Only Difference Is How Much You Spend." *Business
    Insider*, November 12, 2020. https://www.businessinsider.com
    /personal-finance/what-is-fatfire-vs-leanfire-early-retirement
    -fire.

Pfau, Wade D. "Sustainable Retirement Spending with Low Interest
    Rates: Updating the Trinity Study." *Journal of Financial Planning*,
    August 2015. Financial Planning Association. https://www
    .financialplanningassociation.org/article/journal/AUG15
    -sustainable-retirement-spending-low-interest-rates-updating
    -trinity-study.

"Retirement Plan and IRA Required Minimum Distributions FAQs."
    IRS. https://www.irs.gov/retirement-plans/retirement-plan-and
    -ira-required-minimum-distributions-faqs.

"The Shockingly Simple Math Behind Early Retirement." *Mr.
    Money Mustache* (blog), January 13, 2012. https://www.
    mrmoneymustache.com/2012/01/13/the-shockingly-simple
    -math-behind-early-retirement/.

Ware, Bronnie. *The Top Five Regrets of the Dying: A Life Transformed
    by the Dearly Departing*. Carlsbad, CA: Hay House, 2019.

"Warren Buffett, 'Oracle of Omaha,' Criticises Wall Street and
    Praises Immigrants." *Guardian*, February 25, 2017. https://www.
    theguardian.com/business/2017/feb/25/warren-buffett
    -berkshire-hathaway-wall-street-apple-annual-letter.

ABOUT THE AUTHOR

Garrett Gee is the founder and author of the Hacker Mindset, a principled approach to accomplishment and life. He is also the seven-figure founder and owner of Hacker Warehouse, a one-stop shop for computer security equipment.

Beginning his information security career at just fifteen, Garrett worked at Sandia National Laboratories and then the Federal Reserve Bank. In 2013, he turned entrepreneur with Hacker Warehouse, a global provider of computer security products to Fortune 100 firms, governments, and militaries.

Renowned for his expertise in hacking and computer security, Garrett is a sought-after consultant for Hollywood, contributing to the authenticity of hacking scenes in productions like *Sense8*, *Mr. Robot*, *Jason Bourne*, and *Jack Ryan*.

Garrett's insights have been highlighted by major international news outlets like CNN, *Bloomberg Businessweek*, *WIRED*, and the *Wall Street Journal*. He is a frequent speaker at prestigious information security conferences such as DerbyCon, ToorCon, and the IEEE Symposium on Secrecy and Privacy.

Register your purchase and get access
to a Hacker Mindset Resource Kit:

HackerMindsetBook.com/register

For more about the author, visit :

GarrettGee.com

Have a question about the book, speaking
engagements, coaching, or mentoring?
Did you find a spelling mistake or
other correction needed? Email:

team@thehackermindset.com